D0567356

## DATE DUE

AUG 1 0 2001

MAY 1 1 2002

WID

BRO
DAR   Printed in U.S.A.

AN

INTRODUCTORY

TRANSFORMATIONAL

GRAMMAR

Prentice-Hall International, Inc., *London*
Prentice-Hall of Australia, Pty. Ltd., *Sydney*
Prentice-Hall of Canada, Ltd., *Toronto*
Prentice-Hall of India Private Limited, *New Delhi*
Prentice-Hall of Japan, Inc., *Tokyo*

Bruce L. Liles
University of Missouri, St. Louis

# AN

# INTRODUCTORY

# TRANSFORMATIONAL

# GRAMMAR

Prentice-Hall, Inc., *Englewood Cliffs, N.J.*

For Robert W. Ackerman

© 1971 by Prentice-Hall, Inc. Englewood Cliffs, New Jersey. All rights reserved. No part of this book may be reproduced in any form or by any means without permission in writing from the publisher.

13-502294-0 (C)
13-502286-X (P)

Library of Congress Catalog Card Number: 70–122388

Printed in the United States of America.

Current printing (last number):

10 9 8 7 6 5 4 3 2

TEXAS WOMAN'S UNIVERSITY
LIBRARY

# PREFACE

Ten years ago a person could read most of the important works in linguistics in a few months, and the scholar could afford to buy most of them for his library. Since that time research in all phases of linguistics has progressed so rapidly that scholars who have been keeping up with developments in their discipline are finding it difficult to read all the relevant works published each year. The person wanting to begin a study of linguistics is overwhelmed by the amount of material available, much of it far too technical for him to understand. The present book is directed toward this person, and it is limited in scope to English transformational grammar.

The student of transformational grammar needs both theory and applications. This book attempts to fuse the two. Also, it shows the reader that there are still many aspects of the English language that are poorly understood and that are being investigated. The exercises at the end of the chapters allow the reader to work with the material that has been discussed and to use the techniques he has learned.

I would like to express my gratitude to the people who helped me in writing this book: to David H. Grady, who suggested that I write it and who worked with me in the initial stages of production; to Frances Cassel and James Foster, who read the manuscript and offered useful suggestions; to Wanda Giles, who proofread the final copy. It would be impossible to list all the books and articles in journals that have affected my thinking; their influence is found on almost every page of this book.

v

# CONTENTS

part one

*PHRASE STRUCTURE*

# chapter one
# GRAMMARS OF ENGLISH

## TRADITIONAL GRAMMAR

Until the sixteenth century, Latin was the primary language of scholarship in England and the rest of Western Europe. The only grammars studied in English schools, therefore, were Latin grammars, which were designed to give Englishmen the skills needed to read, write, and sometimes converse in this lingua franca of Western Europe. During the sixteenth and seventeenth centuries, grammars of English began to appear. Since these early grammars were studied exclusively as an aid to learning Latin, they rigorously followed Latin models, although the structure of English is quite different from that of Latin.

For an example of differences between these languages, we can look at how they indicate such relationships as performer and receiver of action. In Latin these relationships are expressed primarily by the forms of the words. In the sentence **Puer virum videt**, "The boy sees the man," we know that **puer**, "boy," is the one performing the act and **virum**, "man," is the one receiving it because there is no ending on **puer**, but -**um** is added to **vir** to give **virum**. The sentence would mean the same thing if the word order were reversed: **Virum puer videt.** To alter the meaning, one must change the *forms* of the words, not their *order*; hence, **Vir puerum videt** means "The man sees the boy," since **vir** has no ending and **puerum** ends in -**um**. In contrast, by the sixteenth century English was relying exclusively on word order to indicate these relationships. The sentence **The boy sees the man** shows that the boy is the performer because the word **boy** precedes the verb; the man is the receiver, since **man** follows the verb. A change in word order produces a change in meaning (**The man sees the boy**) or a meaningless sentence (**Sees the man the boy**). Logically, a grammar of Latin should discuss the forms of words, whereas one of English should give more emphasis to the order in which they are arranged. The purpose of the

3

early grammars of English, however, was not to provide an accurate description of the language, but rather to serve as a basis for the study of Latin grammar. English word order was largely ignored, and the meaning of such relationships as actor and receiver was emphasized as a preface to Latin forms.

During the Renaissance, Latin was replaced as the language of scholarship by English and the other Western European languages. Because of this new role for English, some Englishmen by the late seventeenth and early eighteenth centuries were greatly concerned with refining their language. They felt that English had somehow become "corrupt" and that it was in need of purification. Through the use of logic they hoped to return English to an "undefiled" state. With unlimited zeal and imagination but limited knowledge about language change and the history of English, they added the s we now have in island and the b of doubt and debt†; they made other changes based on equally misunderstood etymologies. They reasoned that since a subjective complement means the same thing as the noun it renames, people should say It is I rather than It is me, that one should use the nominative he in Bill wanted to be he but the objective him in Bill wanted it to be him. Unfortunately, they were silent about whether to use the nominative or the objective in We discussed its being ——. By logic this should be We discussed its being my, the possessive my agreeing with its. They reasoned out rules for shall and will, should and would. They legislated against ending sentences with prepositions and against splitting infinitives. These rules were based entirely on logic; no attention was given to what educated people were actually saying. For their classification of words and sentences, they followed the patterns set by grammars of the preceding two centuries.

From this tradition developed the English grammars used in schools during the nineteenth and twentieth centuries. This traditional grammar is best known to many people in the United States from high-school textbooks, college handbooks, *Plain English Handbook* by Walsh and Walsh, and *Descriptive English Grammar* by House and Harmon. It followed Latin grammar in concentrating on parts of speech that are subcategorized according to case, person, number, gender, mood, tense, etc. These concepts are informative in a study of Latin, but many of the categories are hard to justify for English. Word order was usually ignored. Sentences were classified as simple, compound, complex, or compound-complex; clauses were classified as independent, noun, adjective, or adverb; phrases were

---

† English iland was respelled island by analogy with French isle, although the two words are not related etymologically. The b in doubt and debt was added by analogy with Latin dubitum and debitum, although Old French had lost the b in these words before English borrowed them.

prepositional, participial, gerund, or infinitive. Many school grammars used the study of English grammar as nothing more than a background for a study of punctuation, subject-verb agreement, pronoun case forms, and other matters of usage.

## STRUCTURAL GRAMMAR

During the nineteenth century, as scholars began studying and comparing large numbers of languages, many of them radically different in structure from Latin, they saw that traditional grammar was inadequate. Some missionaries and other people describing exotic languages assiduously forced them into the framework of Latin grammar, but others realized the shortcomings of the tradition. This dissatisfaction with traditional grammar continued into the twentieth century, when Jespersen and Poutsma found it necessary to make significant departures from traditional grammar in their monumental works on English.† Many teachers became disillusioned with the grammar they were teaching when they discovered that it would not account for many ordinary sentences that are encountered in modern newspapers and magazines; for exercises they were limited to carefully selected sentences in their texts. They often found that in their teaching they were relying more upon observations they had made about the language than upon explanations in the texts.

Discontent with traditional grammar grew to such proportions that during the second quarter of the twentieth century a new approach to the study of language evolved: *structural linguistics*. Followers of this approach felt that it was necessary to study the structure of a language as objectively as possible without reference to any other language, and they felt that meaning was a poor guide to the analysis of structure. Instead of talking about what a noun means ("the name of a person, place, or thing"), for example, they began looking for other devices to identify nouns. In a sentence such as **The arguments became heated**, they said that the word **arguments** can be recognized as a noun because it has a plural ending, because it has the suffix **-ment**, because it follows the determiner **the**, and because it precedes the verb **became**. They attempted to analyze other grammatical elements in terms of *structure* rather than *meaning*.

---

† Otto Jespersen, *A Modern English Grammar on Historical Principles*, 7 vols. (Copenhagen: Ejnar Munksgaard, 1909–1949). H. A. Poutsma, *A Grammar of Late Modern English* (Groningen: P. Noorhoff, 1914–1926). Jespersen and Poutsma belong neither with the traditional grammarians discussed in the preceding section nor with the structuralists. Gleason in his *Linguistics and English Grammar* (New York, 1965) calls them "scholarly traditional" grammarians.

The structuralists based their conclusions upon analyses of sentences that they had collected from native speakers of English. One of the most remarkable of the structuralists was Charles C. Fries, who obtained access to letters written to a government agency as a corpus for his analysis presented in *American English Grammar* (New York: Appleton-Century-Crofts, 1940). Later he obtained permission to record telephone conversations, unknown to the people talking. The results of this study were published in *The Structure of English* (New York: Harcourt, Brace and World, 1952). Because of Professor Fries' integrity and efficiency, access to the materials was carefully controlled. The illustrative material in the published results of the studies had all names replaced by dashes, and sentences that could identify the speaker because of their content were carefully excluded. Professor Fries' work was widely read and emulated by later structuralists such as Francis, Hill, and Stageberg.†

The work of the structuralists brought attention to the word *linguist*, a term that had previously been used to designate someone who studied languages, particularly someone who spoke several different languages. But after the publication of Leonard Bloomfield's *Language* in 1933, the term *linguist* became specialized to mean only the person concerned with the new scientific study of language. The word *linguistics* became popular as the name of his discipline. Until the late 1950's, the terms *structuralist* and *linguist* were practically synonymous in America. The structuralists made many praiseworthy contributions to the study of language. They challenged current attitudes and began the scholarly study of language that has rapidly increased during the last two decades.

## TRANSFORMATIONAL GRAMMAR

Starting formally in 1957 with the publication of Noam Chomsky's *Syntactic Structures*, a new approach to the study of language was inaugurated. This newer grammar has gone under various names: *generative, transformational, generative-transformational*, and *transformational-generative*. This is the kind of grammar presented in this book, and the term *transformational* is used for consistency and brevity. Scholars have been so impressed by the importance and potential of transformational grammar that since 1957 the majority of published studies of English syntax have used this approach. During the

† Archibald A. Hill, *Introduction to Linguistic Structures* (New York: Harcourt, Brace and World, 1958). W. Nelson Francis, *The Structure of American English* (New York: The Ronald Press Company, 1954). Norman C. Stageberg, *An Introductory English Grammar* (New York: Holt, Rinehart and Winston, Inc., 1965).

past ten years there have been many developments in transformational grammar, and there will certainly be more in the future. Almost every aspect of language is still being examined. There is so much controversy among linguists that many people use the plural in speaking of *transformational grammars*; there is no single transformational grammar which is accepted by all scholars in the field. Nevertheless, there are many ideas which most transformationalists do accept.

The transformational grammarian is not content with describing what he finds in a corpus of sentences collected from native speakers. He feels that his grammar should enable one to produce all the sentences of a language, and he is as interested in possible sentences as he is in the ones actually recorded. Since the number of possible sentences in English or any other language is infinite, no one could have heard all of them. Yet native speakers of English understand new sentences such as I spilled milk in the bathtub and He left his shoe polish in the refrigerator. Every day the native speaker hears, reads, and creates new sentences, sentences which seem so ordinary that he is not aware that they have never been used before. An adequate grammar of English should enable a person to produce not just those sentences that have been said in the past, but all the sentences that a native speaker is capable of creating or understanding. In addition, the grammar should not generate sentences that a native speaker would reject, such as *The man horrified the door or *Boy on the roof is.

Notice the asterisk in the last two sentences. This mark is used to indicate that a sentence or a part of a sentence is ungrammatical; that is, no native speaker of the language would intentionally use it.† By *grammatical* we are not referring to standard and nonstandard usage. He ain't going is grammatical for some people (there are native speakers who say it), but it is nonstandard (educated speakers do not normally use it). *He not is going is not grammatical, since no native speakers use this construction. Calling sentences like He ain't going and Irregardless of what you think, he taken it grammatical does not mean that the linguist is encouraging anyone to use them when applying for a job. He is merely restricting the meaning of the term *grammatical* to structures that are normally used by native speakers of English. He refers to acceptability among various social groups or in various contexts as *usage*.

The transformationalist is more concerned with the system that underlies the language than he is with the actual speech of an individual at any given time. All speakers occasionally stammer, make false starts, use wrong words, get words out of order, and change constructions in midcourse.

---

† The word *intentionally* is important. Native speakers do make ungrammatical sentences, especially when they are excited or tired. These are normally looked upon as unintentional slips.

In addition, speech may be affected by physical surroundings, emotions, memory limitations, distractions, or other features such as chewing gum in the mouth of the speaker. It is language (the underlying system), not actual speech output, that is of primary interest to the transformationalist. Another way of stating this is to say that he is interested in the speaker's *competence*, or knowledge of the language, rather than in his *performance*, or actual use of it.

In some respects transformational grammar is similar to traditional grammar. Transformational grammar assigns each sentence an underlying structure that is called a *deep structure*. Some traditional grammars used a similar concept in speaking of "understood" elements. For example, they said that Tom is taller than I has the underlying form Tom is taller than I am tall and that imperative sentences such as Come here have an understood subject you. Transformational grammarians agree, but apply this idea of underlying structure to every sentence and express it in a more abstract form than traditional grammarians did.

As transformationalists began studying deep structures, they noticed that languages which are quite different on the surface often show many similar features in their deep structures. Some linguists are now investigating the possibility that there is a universal deep structure underlying all languages. Sentences having this universal deep structure are converted into the sentences of particular languages by a process known as *transformation.*† Although this line of investigation is new and offers almost limitless possibilities for further research, enough discussions of it have been either published or presented as papers at professional meetings to make the idea of a universal deep structure seem plausible. It will probably be several years before we understand universal deep structure well enough to incorporate information about it into an introductory text. A slightly earlier concept has, therefore, been adopted for this text. The term *deep structure* will be used to refer to an English deep structure, not a universal one.

## exercises

A. Make up five sentences that you think you have never heard, read, or said before.
B. Select any book at random and make a list of the sentences you find repeated in it. Set yourself a reasonable time limit or number of pages. What does your list suggest about the number of sentences possible in English?

† The concept of a universal grammar was discussed during the seventeenth and eighteenth centuries and was then ignored for two centuries. Many linguists now regard this early idea as essentially correct. For a discussion of the theories of the seventeenth and eighteenth centuries, see Noam Chomsky, *Cartesian Linguistics* (New York: Harper and Row, 1966).

C. Reread this chapter and mark the sentences you think you have read or heard before. Why were you able to understand the sentences that were totally new to you?

D. Listen to a conversation that you are not actively participating in and find examples of sentences that do not accurately reflect the speaker's competence. Are false starts, incomplete structures, and other mistakes very common? Why do they normally go unnoticed?

E. We could make an analogy to linguistic competence and performance with a student's performance on a test. Show how his performance may not accurately reflect his competence, or knowledge of the subject matter. How many of these interfering factors also prevent a person's performance from accurately reflecting his competence in language?

# chapter two
# THE STRUCTURE
# OF THE SENTENCE

If you examine the sentence Yes, my neighbor has seen the dog, you notice
that the words are arranged in a definite order. Any other arrangement is
ungrammatical:

1. *My neighbor has seen yes the dog.
2. *Yes, neighbor my has seen the dog.
3. *Yes, my neighbor the dog has seen.
4. *Yes, my neighbor seen has the dog.

Because of the obvious importance of word order in English, we will be
calling attention to this process throughout the book.

Not only do the words have a prescribed order, but they also cluster
together in groups within the sentence. My neighbor forms a group, as does
the dog; on the other hand, neighbor has and seen the do not form complete
groups. If we break the sentence into natural groups, the first break will be
between yes and my neighbor has seen the dog. The second group can be
divided into my neighbor and has seen the dog. My neighbor can be
divided into my and neighbor. Sentences in English, then, are formed not
only of words in a specific order, but also of words arranged in hierarchical
groupings, in which words combine to form groups which are in turn parts
of larger groups.

Among these groups my neighbor and the dog seem to be the same
kind of structure since they can substitute for each other:

1. Yes, my neighbor has seen the dog.
2. Yes, the dog has seen my neighbor.

We will use names to label structures so that we can show which ones are similar. My neighbor and the dog are called *noun phrases* since a noun is the chief word in each.†

Almost all fields of study have abbreviations for terms that are often repeated; this grammar is no exception. Instead of writing *sentence* many times in our rules, we use the abbreviation **S**; similarly, *sentence modifier* is abbreviated **SM**, *noun phrase* is **NP**, and *verb phrase* is **VP**. Rules in a transformational grammar are expressed in the following way:

S → (SM) Nuc

Nuc → NP + VP

The arrow means "consists of" or "is to be rewritten as." These rules say that in English a sentence consists of a sentence modifier and a **nucleus**; a nucleus (**Nuc**) consists of a noun phrase and a verb phrase. The parentheses around **SM** mean that this element is optional; i.e., the sentence may or may not contain it. Since Nuc is not in parentheses, every sentence must include a nucleus. Notice that there is no plus mark between parenthesized elements and adjoining elements. In the second rule the fact that NP and VP are not in parentheses indicates that both are necessary for every sentence in English. The rules also indicate the order in which elements must be selected: the sentence modifier must come first, then the nucleus; in the nucleus the noun phrase must come first, then the verb phrase.

A sentence modifier is a word or group of words like yes, no, certainly, naturally, maybe, perhaps, possibly, in fact, to be sure, or obviously. In Yes, that woman drinks coffee, the SM is yes, and the Nuc is that woman drinks coffee; in the Nuc, the NP is that woman, and the VP is drinks coffee. As you may have noticed, *noun phrase* is the name of the structure that functions as the complete subject of a sentence; the *verb phrase* is the structure that functions as the complete predicate. This distinction between structure and function is the same one traditional grammarians were making when they called a word a *noun* or *pronoun* by structure but *subject* or *direct object* by function. In the sentence Of course John snores, the SM is of course and the Nuc is John snores; the NP is John, and the VP is snores. In the sentence John snores, the optional SM has not been selected. Notice that a noun phrase may be a single word (John ran) or a group of words (The little boy ran).

Our use of the word *rule* is different from that used in traditional grammar. A rule for a transformationalist is not an explanation of how to

---

† We are not using the word *phrase* in the same sense that traditional grammarians used it.

punctuate a sentence or how to avoid errors. Rather, it is a direction for forming a sentence or part of a sentence. The rules in a transformational grammar will specify which combinations of words are grammatical sentences.

In addition to rules that generate the sentences of English, we also have a means of representing the exact choices that are made in the derivation of specific sentences. This is known as a **tree**. The sentence **Yes, that man drinks milk** is represented as follows:

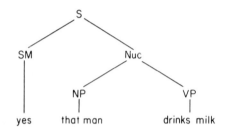

The sentence **That man drinks milk** is represented without the optional element SM:

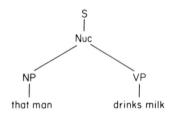

Sentences in English are not composed of mere sequences of words; rather, as we noticed at the beginning of this chapter, they are composed of words that cluster together, often in complex hierarchies. In the above sentence, **that man drinks milk** is one cluster, which in turn is composed of two subordinate clusters: **that man** and **drinks milk**. Notice that the tree shows this arrangement.

Before proceeding to the noun phrase, you should practice drawing a few trees:

1. Certainly, I know the answer.
2. He has gone.
3. The fireman fought the fire.
4. Apparently Tom is sick.
5. Unfortunately the fish died.

All rules in a transformational grammar are numbered: P1, P2, P3, etc. **P** stands for *phrase structure*, the name for this section of the grammar. There will be some skips in the numbers given in the rules at this time, since some of them will not be needed until later in the chapter. Also, some rules will be expanded in later chapters of this book. So far we have two rules:

P1: S → (SM) Nuc

P2: Nuc → NP + VP

A noun phrase always contains a **nominal** (**N**), which may be a pronoun (he, she, we, I, they, you, etc.), a name (John, Mrs. Smith, New York, The Grapes of Wrath, etc.), or a common noun (book, bottle, egg, table, girl, etc.). In Chapter Four of this book we will discuss ways of distinguishing these three kinds of nominals. For now they are all classified as Ns. Some nominals are preceded by **determiners** (**Det**), such as the, a, that, this, these, those, etc.; some nominals may be in the **plural** (**Pl**).

P7: NP → (Det) N (Pl)

The parentheses around Det and Pl mean that these elements are optional. A later section of the grammar will tell us to read book + Pl as books, egg + Pl as eggs, dish + Pl as dishes, deer + Pl as deer, child + Pl as children, etc.

The tree contains all of the information from the rewrite rules for each sentence generated. Here is the representation for Those apples look green:

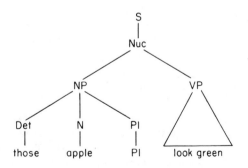

The triangle under VP tells us that no further analysis is being given for look green.

Before proceeding further, draw trees of the following:

1. An apple lay on the ground.
2. Those pearls look genuine.
3. Surely you can go with us.
4. The ducks are noisy.
5. Certainly those sheep ran fast.

Many of the terms used in transformational grammar are similar in meaning to those used in traditional grammar: *subject, article, demonstrative, sentence,* etc. Some of them, such as *determiner* and *noun phrase,* are new. In addition, certain terms from traditional grammar are used by transformationalists but with different meanings. We have already encountered one of these: *verb phrase.* To the traditionalist the verb phrase in the sentence The man must have found the note is must have found; to the transformationalist it is must have found the note. This does not reflect any disagreement between the two schools of thought; they are merely using the same term to refer to different ideas. There will be several other terms that are used with meanings different from those found in traditional grammar.

Let us now examine the components of the verb phrase:

P3: VP → Aux + MV (manner) (place) (time) (reason)

This means that a verb phrase consists of (or "is rewritten as") an **auxiliary** (**Aux**), a **main verb** (**MV**), and optional adverbials of **manner** (rapidly, with ease), **place** (there, at home), **time** (then, at noon), or **reason** (because of the noise). In the sentence The man will drive carefully in town today because of the ice, the Aux is will, the MV is drive, manner is carefully, place is in town, time is today, and reason is because of the ice.

Later we will have a great deal more to say about the English auxiliary, but for the present only one element will be introduced:

P4: Aux → tense

P5: tense → $\begin{Bmatrix} \text{present} \\ \text{past} \end{Bmatrix}$

These two rules say that every auxiliary contains **tense**, and that tense is either present or past. In the sentence The woman sang to me, the tense is past; in The woman sings to me it is present. In They are at home, the tense is present; in They were at home it is past. You will notice that tense is not a separate word, as are the other elements we have been considering. We list gave as *past* + *give* (i.e., "the past tense of give"), gives as *present* + *give*, give (as in We give parties often) as *present* + *give*. Every verb will be preceded by a symbol for tense.

Later when we are discussing transformations, we will need to distinguish between be and other verbs. A few examples will show the reason for this. He was my friend has a related negative form He was not my friend, in which the word not is found after was, a past form of be. The related negative of He saw my friend does not follow this pattern. Instead of *He saw not my friend, which would be parallel to He was not my friend, in Modern English we say He didn't see my friend, with the addition of do. Similarly, in questions we find a difference between be and other verbs. He was my friend has the related form Was he my friend? He saw my friend does not have as its related form *Saw he my friend? but rather Did he see my friend?

$$P6: \text{MV} \rightarrow \left\{ \begin{array}{l} \text{be} \left\{ \begin{array}{l} \text{NP} \\ \text{place} \\ \text{AP} \end{array} \right\} \\ \text{V (NP)} \end{array} \right\}$$

This rule says that an MV is to be rewritten as any one of the following structures:

1. be + NP        This book is a text.
2. be + Place     Betty was in the car.
3. be + AP        She was very rude.
4. V              John ran.
5. V + NP         Bill sold the tickets.

Whenever we speak of verbs, we are excluding forms of be (am, is, are, was, were, be, been, being). You can probably think of other structures following verbs, such as Susan seemed happy and We considered Susan lucky. These will be treated in a later chapter.

**AP** is an abbreviation for *adjective phrase*, which consists of an optional **intensifier (Intens)** such as very, extremely, rather, etc. and an **adjective (Adj)** such as old, happy, green, etc. Here is the rule:

P8: AP → (Intens) Adj

If we were writing a complete grammar of English in which we were trying to describe all details, we would include many more rules. For example, we could distinguish among the following kinds of adverbials:

1. The adverb (rapidly, cheerfully, lengthwise).
2. The prepositional phrase (in the yard, at school, over the fence).
3. The uninflected word (here, there, today).
4. The noun phrase (as in We walked a mile).

Since this book is intended only as an introduction to transformational grammar rather than an exhaustive grammar of English, we will use the terms *manner*, *place*, *time*, and *reason* for any of these structures. They function alike in the rules that follow.

In case you are having trouble classifying the words following verbs as noun phrases, adverbs, etc., a few suggestions may be helpful. Only a noun phrase may contain a determiner or be in the plural. In the sentence John turned the wheel, we know that the wheel is a noun phrase because of the determiner the; also, we would not be altering the structure if we changed wheel to wheels. Some nouns do not have plural forms: She drank the milk. There is no such form as *milks with this meaning: *She drank the milks. As you will see in Chapter Four, many abstract nouns and proper nouns do not take determiners or plural endings: John admires courage. You will learn to recognize these nouns with practice. Except for a few obvious proper nouns and pronouns, all the noun phrases in the exercises following this chapter are readily recognizable by the presence (or possibility) of determiners and plurals.

An adjective phrase may contain an intensifier: They were rather friendly; They are stubborn. In the first sentence, rather friendly is recognizable as an adjective phrase because of the intensifier rather. In the second sentence, stubborn is an adjective phrase because it could be preceded by an intensifier such as very. Also, friendly and stubborn may be compared: friendlier and more stubborn.

Some adverbials may also be accompanied by intensifiers or be compared, but not adverbials of place: They are here, but not *They are very here or *They are more here. Adverbials of place may be replaced by here or there: They were in the kitchen or They were there. Most adverbials of place are prepositional phrases, and prepositional phrases *contain* noun phrases, such as the kitchen in the above sentence. In classifying structures, do not be concerned with elements contained within the one you are examining. To the bank in We went to the bank is a prepositional phrase used as an adverbial of place; we can substitute there for it. It is irrelevant that it contains a noun phrase. Another way of stating this is to say that **the bank** is a noun phrase, but that **to the bank** is a prepositional phrase used as an adverbial of place.†

We can incorporate all of the information contained in our rewrite rules in trees:

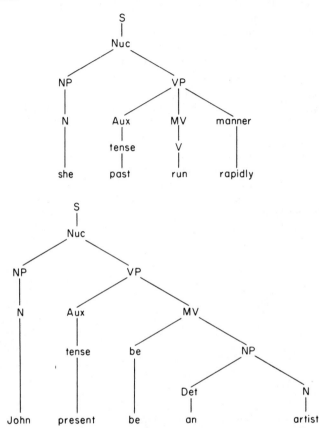

Notice that the tree shows the structure of the sentence. We call each of the places at which a symbol is written a *node* and say that a node *dominates* anything connected by lines below it. From the tree we can see that **John** is an N, since the N node dominates it. Similarly, **an** is a Det, **be an artist** is an MV, **present be an artist** is a VP, etc. On the other hand, **John present be** is not dominated by any single node and is, therefore, not a structural unit.

† Some grammars would list **to the bank** as an adverbial of direction. In this text we will not be distinguishing between place and direction, since they are both replaced in questions by **where**.

## exercises

A. Draw trees of the following sentences:
  1. The boy ate a hamburger greedily.
  2. Bobby is quite intelligent.
  3. Of course, the car is in the garage.
  4. Naturally those ducks sat there for an hour.
  5. No, those women planted the garden yesterday.

B. Without thinking of any particular sentence, begin with rule P1 and work through the rewrite rules until you can no longer rewrite anything. When you are allowed a choice, select any of the alternatives at random. Then select words that will fit the structure you have produced.

C. Some traditional grammars point out that many adverbs end in -ly and answer the question **how.** To which class of adverbs do these criteria apply? According to this information, what part of speech should **sickly** be in **She was sickly most of the time**? If -ly is added to a noun, such as **love, friend,** or **heaven,** is the result an adverb? What part of speech normally results from -ly added to an adjective, such as **sudden, careful,** or **peaceful**? Are adverbs the only words that answer **how**?

# chapter three
## *THE AUXILIARY*

The only element in the auxiliary that we have seen so far is tense. We now need to expand our rewrite rule so that it will include such auxiliaries as those in the sentences **We had been eating** and **They must have been looking at us**. The sentences in the left column below contain nothing but tense in the auxiliary; those in the right column have had something added to them. Analyze these expanded sentences to see what has been added:

1. The bird sings.     The bird is singing.
2. The bird sang.     The bird was singing.
3. I eat sandwiches.     I am eating sandwiches.
4. I ate sandwiches.     I was eating sandwiches.

In the sentences on the left, tense is attached to the main verb: **sings** (present) and **sang** (past), **eat** (present) and **ate** (past). In the sentences on the right, however, the main verb does not change with variations in tense; it remains **singing** or **eating**, regardless of which tense is selected. Variation in tense is shown, rather, in the auxiliary, which is a form of **be**: **is singing** (present) and **was singing** (past), **am eating** (present) and **was eating** (past). Along with this form of **be** that has been added to the auxiliary there is another **morpheme** (a unit that cannot be broken into smaller grammatical units): the present participial **ing**. This morpheme is attached to the word that immediately follows the auxiliary **be**: **is singing, was eating**. We can now make the first of several expansions of the auxiliary:

P4: Aux → tense (be + ing)

This means that every auxiliary contains tense. The elements **be** and **ing** are optional, but if they are chosen, both must be selected and they must come in this order, following tense. **Ing** is attached to the word that follows it. By **ing** we are not indicating the pronunciation of this morpheme; we are simply using it as a symbol for *present participle*. The tree for **She is singing** looks like this:

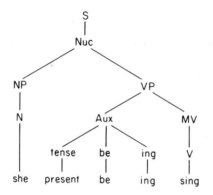

Now examine the following pairs of sentences. Again, those on the left have just tense in the auxiliary, but those on the right have been expanded:

1. We take medicine.        We have taken medicine.
2. We took medicine.        We had taken medicine.
3. Ann drinks milk.         Ann has drunk milk.
4. Ann drank milk.          Ann had drunk milk.
5. I am here.               I have been here.
6. I was here.              I had been here.
7. He has the answer.       He has had the answer.
8. He had the answer.       He had had the answer.

Again, you will notice that with the addition of some element in the auxiliary besides tense, the tense morpheme is no longer attached to the main verb, but rather to the other auxiliary: **have** or **has** (present) versus **had** (past). For the time being forget about time in relation to tense; we shall have more to say about that later. Since the only change in *form* that can be made in **have taken** or **has taken** is to **had taken**, we say that **have taken** and **has taken** contain the present-tense morpheme, **had taken** the past-tense morpheme. Instead of **be** + **ing**, this time we have added a form of **have** in the auxiliary, and with it we have added **en** (the past-participial morpheme) to the following word (**taken, drunk, been, had** in the sentences above). We represent this morpheme with the symbol **en** regardless of the actual form of the past participle. *En* + *eat* is **eaten**, *en* + *hear* is **heard**, *en* + *drink* is **drunk**, *en* + *hit* is **hit**, etc. By **en** we are not indicating the pronunciation of any part of the past participial form of any verb; it is merely a convenient, short symbol so that we do not have to write **past participle of** each time we use it. We could now rewrite rule P4 as follows:

Aux → tense (*have* + *en*)

The only reason we do not is that we have already seen that *be* + *ing* may also be part of the auxiliary.

We know that either *be* + *ing* or *have* + *en* may exist between tense and the verb. We now need to see whether they are mutually exclusive or whether both may be selected for the same auxiliary. Examine the following sentences:

1. They had been singing songs.
2. They have been singing songs.
3. She has been smiling at me.
4. She had been smiling at me.
5. *She was having smiled at me.
6. *They are having sung songs.

It is obvious that both *be* + *ing* and *have* + *en* may exist in the same auxiliary. When both are present, *have* + *en* comes first. Tense is attached to **have**. We can expand rule P4 like this:

Aux → tense (*have* + *en*) (*be* + *ing*)

This means that every auxiliary must contain tense. An auxiliary may contain both the other pairs of elements, one of them, or neither. If **have** is selected, then the next word must contain the morpheme **en**; if **be** is selected, the next word must contain **ing**. Whichever elements are selected, they must come in the order in which they are listed in the rewrite rule. Tense is attached to the element that immediately follows it. Here is a tree for a structure in which both **have** and **be** have been selected as auxiliaries:

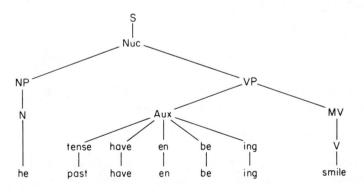

The past form of have is had, the en form of be is been, and the ing form of smile is smiling; the sentence is He had been smiling.

We need to make one final addition to the auxiliary. Examine the following sentences:

1. I can give the answer now.
2. I could give the answer yesterday.
3. They will stop soon.
4. They would stop soon.
5. She may be joking.
6. She might be joking.
7. We shall be leaving.
8. We should have been leaving.
9. You must be going.

These sentences have their auxiliaries expanded by the addition of the following words: can, could, will, would, may, might, shall, should, must. You should recognize the other elements of the auxiliary: *have* + *en* and *be* + *ing*. We call these new words **modals** and use the abbreviation **M** for them. Notice that modals precede other auxiliaries and that the word following a modal is in the uninflected (or infinitive) form.

In Modern English, tense with modals presents a problem. In earlier English, can, will, may, and shall were present-tense forms and could, would, might, and should (notice the d or t) past-tense forms. In a few structures, such as I can do it now and I could do it yesterday, the tense distinction is still evident, although the idea of time is more firmly expressed by the adverbials now and yesterday than by the verb. But such obvious distinctions are rare today. Most sentences with modals, in fact, seemingly do not contain tense in referring to time, and we could probably justify a rule saying that an auxiliary contains tense *or* a modal, giving our rewrite rule for the auxiliary as:

$$\text{Aux} \rightarrow \left\{ \begin{array}{c} \text{M} \\ \text{tense} \end{array} \right\} \ (have + en) \ (be + ing)$$

But such a rule ignores the tense relationship that does exist between such pairs of sentences as I can do it now and I could do it yesterday. We will, therefore, continue to use a rule that has become accepted:

P4: Aux → tense (M) (*have* + *en*) (*be* + *ing*)

Regardless of meaning, classify the following modals as present: may, can, will, shall, must; these as past: might, could, would, should.

For most verbs all combinations of the auxiliary are possible. There are some nonaction verbs, however, that do not exist with be + ing: seem, hear, know, hate, understand, etc. (*She was seeming frightened). The copula be as in He was a nuisance does not take the auxiliary be + ing, although there is another verb be (He was being a nuisance) which expresses action. This feature will be treated as a peculiarity of certain verbs and will be included in their dictionary entries. We do not need to change rule P4 for these exceptions.

Here is a tree for the sentence He could have been running. It contains the maximum expansion of the auxiliary.

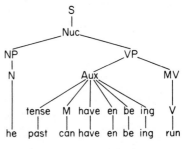

You have probably wondered about our treatment of tense in some sentences. We have said that He has seen us contains present tense, but He had seen us contains past tense. It is obvious that both sentences describe action that occurred during past *time*. Also we have called the tense in He will go present and He would go past, although they both clearly indicate future time. In fact, we have not even mentioned a future tense.

Traditional grammar lists three basic tenses. It defines present tense as an expression of action occurring at the present time, past tense as action occurring during the past, and future tense as action occurring during future time. These tenses are represented by the following forms of the verb: I see (present), I saw (past), I shall see (future). In addition, there are three perfect tenses, indicating completed action and formed by the addition of have + en to the auxiliary. Many traditional grammars stop with these six tenses; but others add three progressive tenses, which indicate continuing action and are formed by the addition of be + ing to the auxiliary. Traditional grammars generally assume that there is a strict correspondence between time and the form of the verb in English.

Such a correspondence does not exist in actual usage. Present time may be represented by the present-tense form of the verb as in Now I understand or Here comes Sally, but it is usually represented by the present progressive form: He is sleeping; They are leaving now; I am eating. For politeness we sometimes use "future tense" for a present action, as a check-out clerk may say, "That will be $6.50, please." The normal meaning of the present-tense form is not present time, but rather action that is habitual or universally true (i.e., past, present, and future time): Tim is a policeman; Water freezes at thirty-two degrees; I eat lunch at one o'clock every day. For many verbs it is impossible to state an action occurring specifically in the present time with the simple present tense: *I eat the cake now (cf. I eat cake often and I am eating the cake now).

Past time is normally expressed by past tense: John ran to town; He had already finished when I came in; In those days I ate a big dinner. But sometimes present tense is used to express past action, as I see that he has been defeated, or When Benjy hears the golfer cry, "Here, caddie," he begins crying, or Europe enters a renaissance during the twelfth century (the historical present). The present perfect tense reflects past time in spite of its name: He has gone; We have finished.

Future time is as often expressed by other means as it is by will and shall; in fact, it may be expressed by any modal or by any tense except past, with adverbials such as tomorrow indicating the time.

1. We leave for New York tomorrow. (Present)
2. If she stays, we must leave. (Present)
3. Ask her if she will stay. (Future)
4. Ask her if she is going to stay. (Present progressive)
5. He has his chance tonight. (Present)
6. He is leaving soon. (Present progressive)
7. When she comes, we'll leave. (Present; Future)
8. He is about to go. (Present)
9. She is to accompany him. (Present)
10. What would you do if you had a flat tonight? (Past)

No one denies the existence of past, present, and future time. We do say that the forms of verbs and auxiliaries in English are not so consistently related to these three times as are the forms of the Latin verb. Time in English is often expressed by other means than the tense of the verb. By *form* there are only two tenses in English: present and past. Remember that by tense we mean the form of the first auxiliary that follows the symbol tense. If there is no such auxiliary, then tense is shown by the form of the main verb. Tense is a concept of form, not meaning.

Elaborate rules for the use of shall, will, should, and would have been devised by earlier textbook writers. The rules first appeared in the seventeenth century and have been perpetuated with embellishments to the present day. Many writers of high-school English texts and of college handbooks are notorious for merely copying rules that have become traditional and never questioning their validity. Most of these texts say that shall and should are normally used for first person, will and would for second and third persons. To show determination, one is to reverse this order, using will and would in first person, shall and should in second and third. Then there are many other rules that vary from text to text, such as the one requiring shall in the question Shall you be here tomorrow? since the anticipated answer is I shall.

These rules offer a good example of the utter futility of trying to legislate English usage. In spite of assiduous drill by schoolmarms for two centuries, the rules have never been followed by many educated people. Most of the better books on usage today have adopted the more sensible approach of describing what educated people actually say, rather than trying to prescribe rules that seem "logical" or "in good taste" to someone while he is thinking about language in his study. It is true that in spoken British English shall and shan't do occur often with first person pronouns. In spoken American English, however, shan't is almost never heard, and shall appears formal, emphatic, or even affected.

No doubt the main reason for the infrequent use of shall in spoken American English is that this modal did not become widely used in London English until after most of the English speaking settlers of what is now the United States had emigrated. The later rise in popularity of shall in England did not spread to this country. Also, in American English both shall and will in speech are contracted in sentences that are not given particular emphasis. I'll go is the normal spoken form, with I will go or I shall go showing either formality or emphasis. In fact, shall because of its infrequent occurrence stands out in spoken American English and gives emphasis or determination for all persons, as McArthur's "I shall return" clearly indicates. The only unemphatic use of shall in spoken American English is in questions like Where shall we sit? and Shall we dance? But even these are now being replaced by such forms as Where would you like to sit? and Would you like to dance? Except for the emphatic form, shall is rarely found in spoken American English.

In formal American English, usage is divided among educated speakers between shall and will for first person. Although I shall and we shall occur frequently in formal written English, it is not at all unusual to find I will and we will in articles in professional journals and in formal correspondence from English professors in leading American universities and from editors of major publishing firms, particularly when rapport with the reader is especially desirable.

Should, like shall, is used differently in British and American English. In unpretentious American speech, should always means "ought to." To most Americans, I should be glad to have you visit me either sounds affected or seems to indicate reluctance. In formal writing, the same practice is observed. Would with first person as in I would be glad to hear from you is the usual form.

## exercises

A. Draw trees of the following sentences:
1. Mabel might be upstairs.
2. Evidently he had read the report reluctantly.

   3. That man must have lacked courage.
   4. The members would have chosen the leader then.
   5. Harold might have been sitting in his room.
   6. He will be a minister next year.
   7. Yes, Murphy has been very quiet.
   8. The firemen will be having trouble soon.

B. After each of the following formulas there are three sentences that may or may
   not have the structure described by the formula. If a sentence follows the
   notation given, write *correct* beside it. If it does not follow this notation, write
   the formula that it does follow.

   1. NP + present + M + V + NP
      a. The student should use the library.
      b. The car will hit the child.
      c. He can sing the song.
   2. NP + past + M + have + en + be + place
      a. The cow has been in the field.
      b. They should have been eating.
      c. People could have been running in the rain.
   3. NP + present + have + en + V + NP
      a. We will have caught him.
      b. They have chosen John.
      c. We are electing him.
   4. NP + past + M + be + NP
      a. He is the owner.
      b. Everybody has gone home.
      c. They would have been conservatives.
   5. NP + present + M + have + en + be + ing + V + place
      a. John is in the barn.
      b. Jack will have been running in the house.
      c. She must have been ill.

C. Write the formula for each of the sentences below, make the addition or deletion
   that is called for, and write the resulting sentence. Example:
   Sally was playing. NP + past + be + ing + play
   Add *have* + *en:* NP + past + have + en + be + ing + play
   Sally had been playing.

   1. I ate then. (Add *be* + *ing*)
   2. They drank the wine. (Add *will*)
   3. We had gone to the window. (Delete *have* + *en*)
   4. You could have listened to me. (Add *be* + *ing*)
   5. They might be disappointed. (Delete *may*)
   6. Sam was telling a lie. (Add *have* + *en*)
   7. You could have been repairing the clock. (Delete *be* + *ing*)
   8. I was going. (Add *shall*)
   9. I could see him well. (Delete *can*)
   10. The waitress must be laughing at us. (Add *have* + *en*)

# chapter four
# *LEXICAL FEATURES*

## *DIVISIONS OF A*
## *TRANSFORMATIONAL GRAMMAR*

In the last two chapters we developed the phrase-structure rules for English. These rules begin with a single symbol S and progress through ordered expansions until no further expansions are possible. The rules are repeated below:

P1: S → (SM) Nuc

P2: Nuc → NP + VP

P3: VP → Aux + MV (manner) (place) (time) (reason)

P4: Aux → tense (M) (have + en) (be + ing)

P5: Tense → $\left\{ \begin{array}{l} \text{present} \\ \text{past} \end{array} \right\}$

P6: MV → $\left\{ \begin{array}{l} \text{be} \left\{ \begin{array}{l} \text{NP} \\ \text{AP} \\ \text{Place} \end{array} \right\} \\ \text{V (NP)} \end{array} \right\}$

P7: NP → (Det) N (Pl)

P8: AP → (Intens) Adj

27

By starting with rule P1 and progressing in order through the rules, selecting or rejecting optional elements, we may expand S in the following way:

S

P1      **Nuc**

P2      **NP + VP**

P3      NP + **Aux + MV**

P4      NP + **tense + be + ing +** MV

P5      NP + **present +** be + ing + MV

P6      NP + present + be + ing + **V + NP**

P7      **Det + N +** present + be + ing + V + NP

P7      Det + N + present + be + ing + V + **Det + N**

P8      Does not apply

There are no longer any symbols that can be rewritten since nothing in the final line occurs to the left in any of our rewrite rules. Symbols such as Det, N, or present that cannot be rewritten by the phrase-structure rules are called *P-terminal symbols*. A sequence, or string, of these symbols is called a *P-terminal string*. A P-terminal string such as

Det + N + present + be + ing + V + Det + N

describes the structure that underlies a grammatical sentence of English, but it is not itself a sentence. It is merely a string of elements, some of which may be out of order and none of which are in their phonetic shape. The phrase structure also tells how the elements in the P-terminal string relate to each other; in other words, it specifies a structure, as exemplified by this tree:

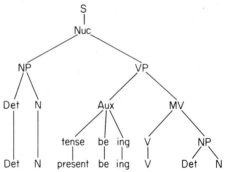

Included in the phrase-structure section of the grammar is a **lexicon** or dictionary, from which we replace such elements as N and V with words:

Det + N + present + be + ing + V + Det + N

The + boy + present + be + ing + read + a + book

These, of course, are not the only words we could have chosen for this structure; the following choices are among the many others that could have been made:

1. A secretary is mailing the letter.
2. The painter is painting the house.

We next proceed to the *semantic* section of the grammar to provide a meaning for the structure. The lexicon will have given meanings for the individual words. The semantic section will tell us how these meanings are combined to provide a meaning for the sentence as a whole. Since very little is known about how the semantic component works, it will not be discussed further in this book.

The phrase-structure rules do not generate finished sentences of English. In fact, they provide only a small number of elementary structures that underlie the sentences of English. To rearrange, delete, or add structures, we need *transformational* rules. For example, we can provide a rule for the structure:

the boy present be        ing read a book

that rearranges it as follows:

present be the boy        ing read a book

This is the order for the question **Is the boy reading a book?** The rearranged structure is illustrated by this tree:

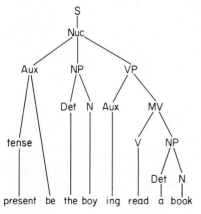

Such transformational rules will be discussed in detail in the next two parts of this book.

Even with the application of transformational rules, we still do not have a grammatical sentence of English. Another set of rules is needed: *phonological* rules that tell us how to pronounce the string that we have generated. These rules will be discussed in Part Four, and they will tell us how combinations of words are pronounced; for example, *present + eat* is **eats,** *past* + *drop* is dropped, etc. (Notice that inflectional morphemes, such as past, en, and ing, remain before the verbs since they are merely symbols, not phonetic representations.) After we apply these rules and those for the addition of stress and pitch, we have a sentence: *Is the boy reading a book?*

We are describing rules that will enable us to produce the sentences of English. We call this collection of rules a *grammar*. The grammar is organized into three sections or components:

1. The syntactic component contains the phrase-structure and transformational rules and provides the **structure** of the sentence.
2. The semantic component operates on the P-terminal string after entries from the lexicon have been added and gives the sentence its **meaning**.
3. The phonological component operates on the sentence after all transformations have been applied and gives the sentence its final **form**.

If we have enough rules in each of these divisions, we can generate all of the sentences of English, including all potential sentences that have never been spoken before. But the ideal grammar not only produces all of the grammatical sentences of a language; it produces no ungrammatical ones. The grammar as we have stated it so far would produce such unacceptable structures as 1a, 2a, 3a, and 4a.

1a. *The smoke vanished the table.
 b.  The smoke vanished.
2a. *An event occurred the man.
 b.  An event occurred.
3a. *The man brought.
 b.  The man brought a book.
4a. *He proved.
 b.  He proved his point.

Rule P6 as we have stated it rewrites MV as be plus one of several structures or as V plus an optional NP. Sentences 1a and 2a are ungrammatical because this optional NP has been selected; 3a and 4a are ungrammatical because it has not been selected.

## TRANSITIVE AND
## INTRANSITIVE RESTRICTIONS

The lexical entry for each verb will have to state whether it permits a following noun phrase or not. Vanish and occur will be listed in the lexicon with the feature [ —___ NP ], and bring and prove will be listed with [ +___ NP ]. The underline indicates the position filled by the verb, before an NP. The plus indicates that the verb in question can fill the position; the minus indicates that it cannot. Some other verbs with the feature [ +____ NP ] are **shoot, wax,** and **tear,** as illustrated in the following sentences:

1. He **shot** a rabbit.
2. I **waxed** the car.
3. Someone **tore** the page.

Some verbs with the feature [ +____ NP ] at times have indefinite noun phrases deleted:

1. Larry ate (something).
2. The students wrote (something).
3. He drove (something).

Other verbs like these are **watch, steal,** and **read.** Whether these verbs have a noun phrase following them or not, there is no alteration in meaning. These verbs still have the feature [ +____ NP ] even when the noun phrase is not present. The feature merely states that a noun phrase is permitted after the verb with the meaning given.

One word of caution is in order. The classification of a verb depends upon its meaning in the sentence under consideration. There is a difference in meaning in **He ran fast** and **He ran the store.** We set up **run** in our lexicon as two separate entries, or as two separate words. The entry with the meaning as in **He ran the store** has the feature [ +____ NP ]; the entry with the meaning **He ran fast** does not have this feature, but rather [ −____ NP ]. This distinction may become complicated for verbs whose meanings are metaphorically extended. Notice **fly** in the following sentences:

1. The bird **flew** out of the room.
2. The angry woman **flew** out of the room in a rage.
3. Last week I **flew** in an airplane.
4. Last week I **flew** an airplane.
5. The dust **flew** everywhere.
6. He **flew** off the handle.

We will list **fly** in our lexicon six different times, one for each meaning. Similar metaphoric extensions can be seen in **rise (The sun rose; The boy rose; Prices rose)** and **die (The man died; The car died).**

Verbs with the feature [ —____ NP ] may be followed by nothing or by optional adverbials, as in the following sentences:

1. The nurse was sleeping.    The nurse was sleeping soundly.
2. The boy fell.              The boy fell to the ground.
3. She hurried.               She hurried because of the rain.

Of course, as we said in the preceding paragraph, different lexical entries may have the same form. Hence, **hurry** in **She hurried** is not the same word as **hurry** in **She hurried us off to work**. Some other examples of verbs that do not permit following noun phrases are **vanish, sweat, pause, rise,** and **occur.** These verbs are traditionally called *intransitive* verbs, as opposed to *transitive* verbs, which do take following noun phrases. Many intransitive verbs can on occasion be followed by a noun that is similar in form to the verb: **He slept a deep sleep; He dreamed a dream** (i.e., nouns that traditional grammar called *cognate accusatives*). Since these are apparently the only nouns that may follow these verbs, they do not affect the classification. A complete grammar would probably introduce them by transformational rules.

Some intransitive verbs must be followed by adverbials if the sentence is to be grammatical:

1. We lay there.        *We lay.
2. He lurked outside.   *He lurked.

Unlike the simple intransitive verbs, these must have an adverbial of place following them. Other examples are **lie** (**recline**), **step,** and **glance.** These verbs have the feature [ +____ place ]. The adverbial is not optional. Sometimes to avoid repetition we delete elements that are otherwise essential. *We sneaked, for example, is ungrammatical by itself. It may occur, however, in the context **How did you get past the guard? We sneaked.** Underlying **We sneaked** is the complete sentence **We sneaked past the guard. Past the guard** has been deleted to avoid repetition. This kind of deletion does not affect our classification.

There are also transitive verbs that must have adverbials of place following the noun phrase:

1. He handed the paper to me.   *He handed the paper.
2. She set the book there.      *She set the book.
3  The doctor laid it there.    *The doctor laid it.

These verbs have the feature [ +____ NP place ], meaning that an adverbial of place must follow the NP.

With these features—[ +____ NP ], [ −____ NP ], [ +____ place ], and [ +____ NP place ]—we can account for the native speaker's intuition that sentences such as *We persuaded and *Someone shivered the man are ungrammatical.

## SUBJECT-VERB RESTRICTIONS

Earlier we said that the phrase-structure rules provide P-terminal symbols such as N and V and that we select items from the lexicon that are designated by these symbols. If we select just any N or V, we could produce the following sentences:

1. The man drove a car.
2. An eraser fell to the floor.
3. *A door sneezed.
4. *He surprised my curiosity.

As the last two examples show, we may not select just any noun or verb, but we must impose certain restrictions.

Notice the following sentences:

1. *The coffee prayed.
2. *Those ants talked to me.
3. *The umbrella coughed.

These are all unacceptable because the subject noun phrases are nonhuman and the verbs require human subjects like the following:

1. The woman prayed.
2. Those children talked to me.
3. My uncle coughed.

It is, therefore, relevant to our grammar whether a noun names a human or not. In the lexicon to indicate that a noun represents a human, we will assign the feature [ + human ]; all other nouns will be [ − human ]. Thus, woman, boy, and aunt are [ + human ], and cat, ivy, and door are [ − human ]. Verbs that do not permit nonhuman subjects have the feature [ − [ − human ]____ ]. The underline indicates the position of the verb, after a noun with the feature [ − human ]. Verbs such as pray, talk, faint, worship, complain, praise, acknowledge, and thank will be listed with this feature to limit them to [ + human ] subjects. Other verbs will not be marked for this feature.

We can thus explain why *The door fainted and *The dog praised me are ungrammatical. In children's stories or other imaginative literature, of course, door and dog may become human. Some people will argue that all of the verbs in the last paragraph may have animate nonhuman subjects; normally they do not make this claim for all animals, but only for pets or certain other animals of which they are particularly fond. Rather than extend the features of the verb for these people, it seems better to say that the distinctions human and nonhuman have been erased in certain cases or perhaps that dog, horse, etc., sometimes have the feature [ + human ] (when they are the subjects of verbs such as worship and acknowledge).

The features we have given will account for the grammaticalness of sentences 1a, 2a, and 3a and for the ungrammaticalness of 1b, 2b, and 3b:

1a. The man bit me.
 b. *The street bit me.
2a. A child ran rapidly into the street.
 b. *A rock ran rapidly into the street.
3a. The cook tasted the soup.
 b. *The chair tasted the soup.

However, if we restricted such verbs as bite, run, and taste to human subjects, we would not be able to produce the following sentences:

1c. The horse bit me.
2c. A dog ran rapidly into the street.
3c. The cat tasted the soup.

Since these are grammatical sentences, limiting these verbs to human subjects would be too strong a restriction. Animals as well as humans can bite, run, or taste something. We need, therefore, another classification of nouns that includes humans and animals. Dog, horse, girl, man have the feature [ + animate ]; rose, rug, and rock have [ − animate ]. Verbs that do not permit inanimate subjects have the feature [ − [ − animate ] ____ ].

The need for a final restriction between subjects and verbs can be seen in the following sentences:

1a.  His coat lay on the bed.

 b.  *His curiosity lay on the bed.

2a.  The cake tasted good.

 b.  *Pettiness tasted good.

3a.  An accident occurred.

 b.  *A snake occurred.

4a.  Six hours elapsed.

 b.  *Six dogs elapsed.

Sentences 1b and 2b have abstract subjects with verbs that require concrete subjects; 3b and 4b have concrete subjects with verbs that require abstract subjects. Generally speaking, concrete nouns name objects that can be touched or seen (cat, apple, woman, etc.). Abstract nouns do not (happiness, honesty, courage, etc.). Abstract nouns are not physically located in space. Concrete nouns have the feature [ + concrete ]; abstract nouns have [ − concrete ]. A verb that does not permit abstract subjects has the feature [ − [ − concrete ] ____ ] (sit, rise, lie, etc.); one that does not permit concrete subjects has the feature [ − [ + concrete ] ____ ] (occur, befall, elapse, etc.). A verb such as amaze, which may occur with either concrete or abstract subjects, will not be marked for this feature.

The four features [ − [ − human ] ____ ], [ − [ − animate ] ____ ], [ − [ − concrete ] ____ ], and [ − [ + concrete ] ____ ] will be given in the lexical entries of only those verbs which are restricted as to the kinds of subjects they may follow. Other verbs, such as seem and appear, will be listed without any of these restrictions since they apparently occur freely with concrete or abstract, animate or inanimate, human or nonhuman subjects.

The verb features we have given are illustrative rather than exhaustive. For example, we could have a classification for verbs that require animate objects (surprise, astonish, terrify, frighten, etc.). Or we might group those verbs together that require living subjects: humans, animals, and plants (grow, die, thrive, etc.). Some verbs take only abstract objects (guess, pretend, announce, etc.). A complete classification of this nature would go far beyond the scope of this book.

Some verbs are even more specific: evaporate must have a subject that is a liquid; read and write must have objects pertaining to writing. Other verbs have equally severe limitations on their subjects (disperse, dissolve, corrode, etc.) or their objects (sing, whistle, say, etc.). A complete lexicon would describe these idiosyncracies.

Here are some verbs with their syntactic features as they would be given in a lexicon:

| *admire* | *eat* |
|---|---|
| [ + _____ NP ] | [ + _____ NP ] |
| [ − [ − human ] _____ ] | [ − [ − animate ] _____ ] |
| *seem* | *occur* |
| [ − _____ NP ] | [ − _____ NP ] |
| | [ − [ + concrete ] _____ ] |

## DETERMINER AND NOUN RESTRICTIONS

We have now classified nouns as human or nonhuman, as animate or inanimate, and as concrete or abstract. These features are needed in accounting for restrictions that hold between nouns and verbs. There are also restrictions on which determiners a noun may take:

1a. *I saw bug on floor.
 b. I saw bugs on the floor.
2a. *The honesty is an admirable trait.
 b. Honesty is an admirable trait.
 c. *Honesty is admirable trait.
3a. *The William entered the room.
 b. William entered the room.

To account for the differences between the grammatical and the ungrammatical sentences above, we must discuss additional noun features.

Nouns are either common [ + common ] or proper [ − common ]. The traditional definition of a proper noun as the name of a particular person, place, or thing and of a common noun as any one of a class works in many cases: Joe vs. boy, Omaha vs. city, etc. On the other hand, the names of seasons of the year, which are traditionally considered common nouns and are not capitalized, are as specific as names of the months, which are proper nouns and are capitalized. Also, the devil seems to be as specific as Satan. Normally proper nouns do not take plurals or articles, the word the in such names as The Hague and the Amazon being taken as part of the name and not a determiner. But even here there are problems. No one would question calling Mr. Smith and Mrs. Smith proper nouns, but when we speak of them together as the Smiths, we have added both an article and a plural morpheme. The following sentences also present problems: *The*

*Americans* landed *three Sundays* ago; *A Canadian* has *two Chevrolets*; There are *two Jims* in my room; He is not *the John Smith* who lives next door to me. That there is some real system underlying the distinction common and proper can be seen in a sentence such as Blamp opened the door. The native speaker recognizes Blamp as the name of a person (or pet), although it is a new word to him. Our grammar should be able to draw similar conclusions. No doubt much of our confusion is caused by a too close association of the noun designation proper with an initial capital letter. The differences between common and proper nouns is a subject that needs further research.

Some nouns name objects that can be counted, whereas others do not. The sentence I read a book can be altered without changing the structure to I read two books or three books or four books. Book has both a singular and a plural form, and various numbers can be placed in front of it. We call book a **count noun** and say that it has the feature [ + count ]. In the sentence I drank a glass of water, the word water cannot be made plural, even if we alter the number of other nouns and verbs in the sentence, nor can we add numbers directly in front of the word. Unlike glass in this sentence, water is a noncount noun and has the feature [ − count ]. The following sentences provide further examples of this feature:

1. The **horse** bit me.            [ + count ]
2. Those **doves** flew away.        [ + count ]
3. The horse ate some **oats**.      [ − count ]
4. The ground needs **moisture**.    [ − count ]

It is possible for a noun to be count in one sentence but noncount in another. In the sentence The ground needs water, water exhibits the feature [ − count ]. But in He has seen the waters of the world, it exhibits [ + count ]. The word water does not mean exactly the same thing in the two sentences. Notice how the following sentences vary this feature:

1. He ate two **eggs**.              [ + count ]
2. He got **egg** on his shirt.      [ − count ]
3. He threw me a **stone**.          [ + count ]
4. The house was made of stone.      [ − count ]
5. I spilled a **Coke**.             [ + count ]
6. I spilled a glass of **Coke**.    [ − count ]

Noncount nouns, such as those in the even-numbered sentences above, often seem to mean substance or material (they are often called mass nouns), whereas the count nouns mean the individual items. A dictionary usually lists these meanings separately. We will treat the count noun stone in sentence three as a different lexical entry from the noncount stone in sentence four.

Sometimes a noun is noncount although we could count the items it names. Furniture, for example, in He owns much furniture, is noncount, since we cannot say one furniture, two furnitures, three furnitures, etc. Yet we can count the pieces of furniture. Similarly, sand in He got sand in his shoe is a noncount noun, although we can count grains of sand.

Some abstract nouns are noncount and do not permit determiners or plural morphemes: *The honesty is good; *They have courages. Other abstract nouns, such as idea and trait, are count nouns and take determiners and plural morphemes freely.

The features [ + count ] and [ − count ] determine which determiners may accompany a noun. If the noun is [ − count ], a may not be used: *A happiness was felt; *A furniture was in the room. If the [ − count ] noun is [ − concrete ], normally the, this, and that may not be used: *I felt the sadness; *He was full of that enthusiasm. Nouns that are [ − count] and [ + concrete ] take the freely: The oil is leaking on the furniture. Count singular nouns may take a or the; they may not exist without any determiner: A man sat in the room; *Man sat in room. Count plural nouns may be preceded by the or by no determiner; they may not be preceded by a: The students came in cars; *A students came in a cars.

Features of a noun can be represented in a matrix, in which we have rows of positively or negatively specified features. Below are the features for the boldfaced nouns in the following sentences: Mary loves truth. The woman owns a cat.

|          | woman | Mary | cat | truth |
|----------|-------|------|-----|-------|
| N        | +     | +    | +   | +     |
| common   | +     | −    | +   | +     |
| count    | +     | −    | +   | −     |
| concrete | +     | +    | +   | −     |
| animate  | +     | +    | +   | −     |
| human    | +     | +    | −   | −     |

A matrix such as this contains much redundant inforamtion. When we classify woman as count, concrete, animate, and human, we are giving much obvious information, since all human nouns are necessarily count, concrete, and animate as well. By omitting all redundant information, we can turn our matrices into more useful forms:

|          | *woman* | *Mary* | *cat* | *truth* |
|----------|:-------:|:------:|:-----:|:-------:|
| N        | +       | +      | +     | +       |
| common   | +       | −      | +     | +       |
| count    |         |        |       | −       |
| concrete |         |        |       | −       |
| animate  |         |        | +     |         |
| human    | +       | +      | −     |         |

A complete grammar would contain rules such as one that automatically applies the features [ + animate ] and [ + concrete ] on all nouns with the feature [ + human ]. All features that are predictable by rules are left unspecified in the matrix.

## THE LEXICON

The lexical features that we have presented in this chapter will be included in the lexicon, or dictionary. Although there are still many unanswered questions regarding the form of an ideal lexicon, the kind of information it should contain is clear. First, there will be a citation form of the word, expressed in phonetic notation. Second, the idiosyncratic properties of the word will be given; these will include the features we have presented and all irregularities (the plural of **foot** is **feet**, the past of **sing** is **sang**, etc.). Third, the meanings or definition of the word will be given. The syntactic component of our grammar will make use of the features of the word, and the phonological component will make use of the phonetic citation form and of inflectional irregularities. The semantic component will use the definitions and the features.

Lexical entries will look something like the following:

1. /maus/
   [ − rule M5 ]
   /maus/ + pl → /mais/

$$\begin{bmatrix} + \text{ N} \\ + \text{ common} \\ + \text{ animate} \\ - \text{ human} \end{bmatrix}$$
   a small rodent

2. /maus/
   [ − rule M5 ]
   /maus/ + pl → /mais/

$$\begin{bmatrix} + \text{ N} \\ + \text{ common} \\ + \text{ human} \end{bmatrix}$$
   a timid woman

3. /maus/
   [ − rule M5 ]
   /maus/ + pl → /mais/

$$\begin{bmatrix} + \text{ N} \\ + \text{ common} \\ + \text{ count} \\ + \text{ concrete} \\ - \text{ animate} \end{bmatrix}$$
   a black eye

The direction [ — rule M5 ] tells us not to apply the rule for regular noun plurals, which would yield *mouses. Current dictionaries seem to indicate the plurals for entries two and three as we have given them. This information may be inaccurate; for these uses there may be no plural forms, or the plural may be mouses.

### exercises

A. Use features to explain why the following sentences are ungrammatical:
   1. *The perseverance is a virtue.
   2. *He has read book.
   3. *A birds flew into the room.
   4. *Despair dropped to the floor.
   5. *The eagle prayed for an hour.
   6. *They handed the book.
   7. *We vanished the spot.
   8. *The tree coughed loudly.
   9. *The bread dripped.
   10. *My boss elapsed.

B. Give the features of the boldfaced words:
   1. The **monkey chewed** the **food** slowly.
   2. A **student coughed** loudly.
   3. He **glanced** at the **water**.
   4. **Bob handed** a **ruler** to me.
   5. The **accident occurred** yesterday.

C. Examine the following sentences and decide why some of them are ungrammatical. What generalizations can you make about **much, many, fewer,** and **less**?
   1. Much energy was spent on this project.
   2. Many apples were in the basket.
   3. *Much children were in the room.
   4. *Many dandruff was in his hair.
   5. *He ate less apples than I did.
   6. He has fewer friends than I have.
   7. She has less confidence than Jane has.
   8. *He has fewer poise than I.

part two

*TRANSFORMATIONS I*

# chapter five
# THE NEGATIVE TRANSFORMATION

The phrase-structure rules can produce the structures underlying such sentences as **Those boys might have been swimming in the lake** and **The manager wrote a letter**. They cannot produce such structures as the following:

1. The manager didn't write a letter.
2. Did the manager write a letter?
3. Who wrote a letter?
4. What did the manager write?
5. A letter was written by the manager.
6. Because the manager wrote a letter . . .
7. The letter that was written by the manager . . .
8. The letter written by the manager . . .
9. For the manager to write a letter . . .
10. The manager's having written a letter . . .

All of these structures seem to be related in some way to **The manager wrote a letter**. The same relationships are found in all of them: the manager is the one who performed the act of writing, and a letter is the result of this action. In spite of dfferences in form, there is a similarity in meaning in all the structures. Transformational rules are used to produce these changes in form.

Earlier we listed several sentence modifiers: **yes, no,** etc. To these we add **not,** which distinguishes a sentence such as **John could sing well** from the negative sentence **John could not sing well**. By selecting the SM **not,** we can derive a structure as shown on page 44. This gives **not John past can sing well,** which is not grammatical. It would be grammatical if we changed the word order to **John past can not sing well** (**John could not**

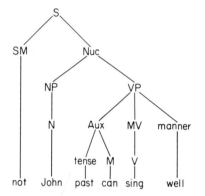

sing well). We now need to introduce two new terms: *deep structure* and *surface structure*. A structure generated only by phrase-structure and lexical rules, such as not John past can sing well, is a deep structure. A deep structure that has been transformed into a grammatical English sentence, such as John could not sing well, is called a surface structure. All grammatical English sentences are surface structures; underlying each one is a deep structure. In later chapters we will modify this statement somewhat. Both deep and surface structures are more abstract than we are presenting them here, since phonological rules have not yet been applied. However, at this stage it is easier to follow the transformational rules if we use a form such as not John could sing well than the abstraction that is the actual deep structure.

All native speakers of English are capable of producing an infinite number of surface structures, or grammatical English sentences. Our purpose is not to teach you how to make negative sentences; any normal five-year old can do that perfectly. Our main purpose in studying these structures is to learn to make accurate observations about how English operates. By *negative* we are referring to sentence negation, not word negation. That is not probable has the SM not. That is improbable does not have this SM and is, therefore, not part of this immediate study, although the processes we are employing in this chapter could easily be extended to account for such negative forms as improbable.

By selecting the optional SM not, we can generate a number of deep structures like those on the left below:

1. not Jerry could hear me          Jerry could not hear me.
2. not Bill has received it          Bill has not received it.
3. not they are going with us          They are not going with us.
4. not they have been doing it          They have not been doing it.

We need to formulate a rule to transform the deep structures on the left to the surface structures on the right. At first glance you might say something like "Move not to the position after the auxiliary." In the first sentence, not Jerry could hear me, this would work, but the third sentence would become *They are ing not go with us (remember that the ing which accompanies the auxiliary be is part of the auxiliary). We must refine our observations. In the surface structure, the negative particle not follows part of the auxiliary, but not all of it. In fact, it follows only the first auxiliary after tense. In not Jerry could hear me, could is a case of *past + can*. Can is the first occurring auxiliary; therefore, not follows it in the surface structure. We use the abbreviation Aux$^1$ for the first auxiliary that comes after tense. In the following sentences Aux$^1$ has been marked:

1. they past can be ing go
2. we present have en eat
3. those dress Pl present must have en be red

So long as the auxiliary contains something besides tense (a modal, have, or be), the first element following tense is Aux$^1$. Our transformational rule for the correct placement of not should read something like this: "Move not to the position following the first auxiliary after tense." Since we will have a number of transformational rules, it will be advantageous to write them in a conventional abbreviated form. The rule can be stated as follows:

$$not + X + tense + Aux^1 + Y \Rightarrow X + tense + Aux^1 + not + Y$$

The information on the left of the arrow describes the structure to which the rule is applicable: one with the SM not and an Aux$^1$. If either of these conditions is not met, the rule does not apply. The information on the right of the arrow describes the structure after the change has been made. The double arrow means that this is a transformational rule rather than a phrase-structure rule. Whereas phrase-structure rules merely expand elements, such as Nuc into NP and VP, transformational rules rearrange, delete, add, or substitute elements, thereby altering the underlying structure of the sentence. The symbol $X$ stands for anything coming between not and tense, such as another sentence modifier or a noun phrase. Since the rule operates the same way regardless of what follows not, we can simplify our rule by using the symbol $X$ for any structure coming between not and tense. Similarly, $Y$ stands for anything following Aux$^1$. This may be other auxiliaries, a verb, and anything that follows a verb. Since the same process applies regardless of what follows Aux$^1$, we can improve the rule by using the symbol $Y$ for this.

For the deep structure not they present can hear you, we can illustrate the rule in the following way:

| not | $X$ | tense | Aux$^1$ | $Y$ | $\Rightarrow$ | $X$ | tense | Aux$^1$ | not | $Y$ |
|-----|-----|-------|---------|-----|---|-----|-------|---------|-----|-----|
| not | they | present | can | hear you | | they | present | can | not | hear you |

This gives They can not hear you, after the phonological rules have been applied. This process can be illustrated with trees. Here is the deep structure:

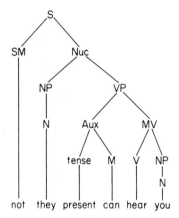

The negative transformation rearranges the tree to provide the following surface structure:

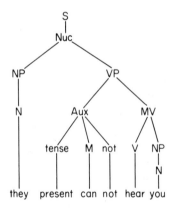

After the application of phonological rules, we have the sentence **They can not hear you.**

Before going further, you should practice with the following structures. Remember that you are trying to understand the process and the mechanics of the rule.

1. not those apples were smelling rotten
2. not Estelle would have done that
3. not you are reading fast enough
4. not Lucille will have finished by then
5. not we had heard the news

Some sentences have only tense in the auxiliary and, therefore, no Aux[1]. For these sentences the rule we have given will not apply. We need to write new rules for these sentences; then we will see how we can modify the rule that we have already formulated. Examine the following deep structures on the left and their corresponding surface structures on the right:

1. not they are our friends        They are not our friends.
2. not Jane was friendly            Jane was not friendly.
3. not the bird was there           The bird was not there.

Like the sentences with Aux[1], these demand a rearrangement of the structure. This time **not** is placed after **be** instead of after an auxiliary. Notice that in these sentences **be** is not an auxiliary, since there is no verb following it and since there is no **ing** on the next word. The **be** in these sentences is part of the MV. We write this rule as follows:

$$\text{not} + X + \text{tense} + \text{be} + Y \Rightarrow X + \text{tense} + \text{be} + \text{not} + Y$$

This rule operates on the following deep structure:

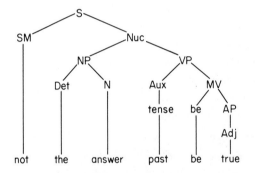

The rule transforms the deep structure into the following surface structure:

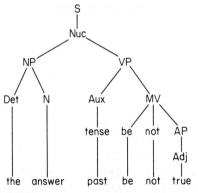

**The answer was not true.**

We have now covered those sentences with some element in the auxiliary in addition to tense; of the sentences with no such auxiliary, we have covered those that contain be as part of the MV. That leaves only those sentences with only tense in the auxiliary and with verbs other than be in the MV. The following structures illustrate the transformation involving these verbs:

1. not we play often              We do not play often.
2. not they taste the salt        They do not taste the salt.
3. not Terry eats early           Terry does not eat early.
4. not the janitor did it         The janitor did not do it.
5. not the man sees me            The man does not see me.

In the surface structure **not** comes before the verb and after tense, which is attached to **do**. If we omit **do** from the surface structure, we obtain the following:

1. We present not play often.
2. They present not taste the salt.
3. Terry present not eat early.
4. The janitor past not do it.
5. The man present not see me.

These are not grammatical sentences, since **not** cannot be altered to show a contrast between past and present. To provide a grammatical sentence, we add the word **do**. Although this word has no lexical meaning, it can carry the tense morpheme: **do** and **does** in contrast to **did**. These sentences require two rules:

$$\text{not} + X + \text{tense} + V + Y \Rightarrow X + \text{tense} + \text{not} + V + Y$$
$$X + \text{tense} + A + Y \Rightarrow X + \text{tense} + \text{do} + A + Y$$

The negative rule moves **not** between tense and the verb. In the second rule, $A$ stands for any morpheme other than an auxiliary or a verb. Any time **tense** appears before any such morpheme, we add the word **do** to carry the tense. To convert the deep structure **not we present jump here** into a surface structure, we apply the negative and *do* transformations as shown in the following trees.

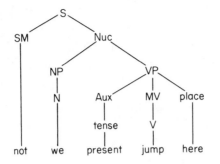

The negative transformation applies to this deep structure to produce the following **intermediate structure**:

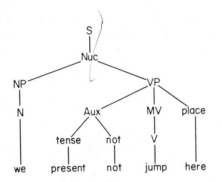

Now the *do* transformation applies to produce a surface structure:

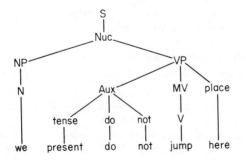

After the application of phonological rules this becomes **We do not jump here.**

We have now given three rules for the negative transformation in English, as follows:

$$\text{not} + X + \text{tense} + \text{Aux}^1 + Y \Rightarrow X + \text{tense} + \text{Aux}^1 + \text{not} + Y$$
$$\text{not} + X + \text{tense} + \text{be} \quad + Y \Rightarrow X + \text{tense} + \text{be} \quad + \text{not} + Y$$
$$\text{not} + X + \text{tense} + V \quad + Y \Rightarrow X + \text{tense} + \text{not} \quad + V \ + Y$$

There is a great deal of repetition among these rules. We have a means of combining the three:

$$\text{not} + X + \text{tense} \begin{bmatrix} \text{Aux}^1 \\ \text{be} \\ V \end{bmatrix} Y \Rightarrow X + \text{tense} \begin{bmatrix} \text{Aux}^1 + \text{not} \\ \text{be} + \text{not} \\ \text{not} + V \end{bmatrix} Y$$

The square brackets indicate that corresponding items must be selected on both sides of the arrow. If Aux$^1$ is selected on the left, then Aux$^1$ + *not* must be selected on the right; if be is selected on the left, then be + *not* must be selected on the right; if V is selected on the left, then *not* + V must be selected on the right.

## exercises

A. Transform the following deep structures into surface structures by applying the negative transformation and, where applicable, the *do* transformation:
   1. not John present be in the room
   2. not of course the children past can go with us
   3. not those chairs present need paint now
   4. not she present look tired
   5. not they present be the leaders
   6. not the boys present will have arrived by then
   7. not no that cat present resemble my sister's cat
   8. not they present have seen me here
   9. not Patsy past be friendly
   10. not his foot past become infected

B. Study the following sentences and determine what governs the use of **some** and **any**:
   1. I read some new magazines. *I read any new magazines.
   2. Some people were at the door. *Any people were at the door.
   3. It isn't in any of the drawers. *It isn't in some of the drawers.
   4. He didn't have any money. *He didn't have some money.
   5. Some dogs were in the yard. *Any dogs were in the yard.

C. Write five original deep structures that contain the SM **not**. Be sure that you can account for all of them with the phrase-structure rules, and use variation in the selection of auxiliary elements. Then transform them into surface structures.

# chapter six
## QUESTION TRANSFORMATIONS

Transformation is the process that converts deep structures into surface structures. The negative transformation involves a rearrangement of structure, as when we move **not** to the position after the first occurring auxiliary or after **be**. In the case of sentences containing only tense in the auxiliary and a verb other than **be**, the word **not** is shifted to the position after tense, and then another transformation adds **do**. This second transformation involves addition, rather than rearrangement of structure. In addition to these two processes, a transformation may delete material from the deep structure:

> He can't sing well, but I can sing well.
> He can't sing well, but I can. (**sing well** is deleted)

Or it may substitute something for a morpheme in the deep structure:

> When Jane saw me, Jane screamed.
> When Jane saw me, **she** screamed.

Some transformations involve a combination of these four processes: rearrangement, substitution, deletion, and addition. Phrase-structure rules do not perform any of these processes; rather, they expand elements (NP, Aux, etc.) into their constituents.

English has two main kinds of questions: those that are answered **yes** or **no** (**Are you ready? Did he leave? Should I stop?**) and those that are answered by other words (**Where are you going? Whose book are you reading? What is her name?**). It will become obvious as we go along that these two kinds of questions are formed differently. We call the first type *yes/no questions*, the second type *WH questions*, since many of them begin with words with the first letters **wh**. In addition, there are questions such as **Sue is going, isn't she?** and **Sue isn't going, is she?** Then there is the echo question: You heard him come in? We will not be treating these kinds of questions, although they can easily be handled by the same processes we use for yes/no and WH questions.

It would be possible to derive yes/no questions from related declaratives such as the following:

1. Tom is sick.               Is Tom sick?

2. They have already left.    Have they already left?

3. He heard us.               Did he hear us?

With this approach we would have the same morphemes in both structures (except for do in Did he hear us?), but the transformation would change the meaning of the sentence. Is Tom sick? does not mean the same thing as Tom is sick. A principle of our grammar is that transformations affect the form of a structure but not the meaning. By means of the negative transformation we derived He will not go from not he will go, both of which have the same meaning. He will not go is not derived from He will go, but is merely similar to it.

Likewise, Tom is sick cannot be the deep structure for Is Tom sick? although the two are similar. Just as the idea of negation must be present in the deep structure of a negative sentence, so the idea of interrogation must be present in the deep structure of a question. This idea is expressed by the SM Q, which indicates that the structure is a question. More specifically, it may be interpreted as meaning "I request that you answer yes or no to the question...."

The sentences on the left below are deep structures that have the sentence modifier Q; those on the right are surface structures:

1. Q she could sing well       Could she sing well?

2. Q the book has become wet   Has the book become wet?

3. Q the bell is ringing now    Is the bell ringing now?

The process of forming questions, like that of making negatives, is not new to you. When you were very young, you incorporated into the grammar that you were learning certain rules for forming questions and negatives. These rules are still part of your grammar, but you are probably not conscious of the intricacies of this grammar, and your observations about it may be inaccurate. You might say that you are moving the verb in front of the subject noun phrase to form a question. This process, of course, would give *Could sing she well? for the first question above, and you would begin refining your observation, as you did in describing the negative transformation. Tense and the first auxiliary (tense + Aux[1]) have been placed in front of the noun phrase in the surface structure; Q has been deleted. This transformation, like the negative, involves a rearrangement of elements. This part of the yes/no rule can be written as follows:

$$Q + NP + tense + Aux^1 + X \Rightarrow tense + Aux^1 + NP + X$$

This rule will apply to a deep structure like this:

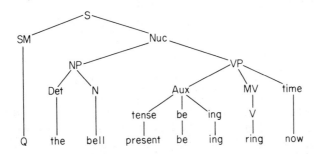

It produces the following surface structure:

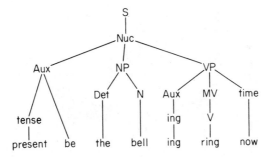

**Is the bell ringing now?**

Now we will examine sentences with no $Aux^1$:

1. Q the men are lucky          Are the men lucky?
2. Q he was our supervisor      Was he our supervisor?
3. Q Betty is at home           Is Betty at home?

When tense is the only element of the auxiliary and the main verb is **be**, the subject noun phrase changes position with tense and **be**, and Q is deleted:

$$Q + NP + tense + be + X \Rightarrow tense + be + NP + X$$

So far we have seen a parallel between this transformation and the negative. Sentences with an auxiliary other than tense behave similarly to sentences with no such auxiliary but with **be** as the main verb. Sentences with only tense as the auxiliary and with verbs other than **be** behave differently under the negative transformation. Let us see whether this parallel is extended to the yes/no transformation:

1. Q John read my letter      Did John read my letter?
2. Q the teachers eat here     Do the teachers eat here?
3. Q she knows my name      Does she know my name?

If we omit the meaningless word **do** from the surface structures, we are left with structures such as **past John read my letter**. When there is no auxiliary other than tense and the main verb is not **be**, tense and the noun phrase change places, so that **Q she present know my name** becomes **present she know my name**. Since **present** cannot be attached to **she**, we apply the **do** insertion rule: **present do she know my name**. These steps can be shown as follows:

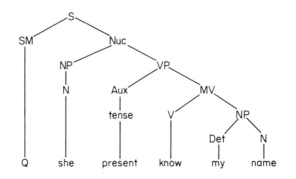

By the yes/no transformation this becomes:

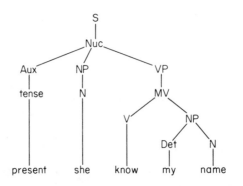

Then *do* insertion applies:

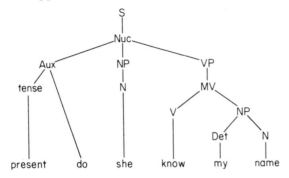

The complete rule for the yes/no transformation can be stated as follows:

$$Q + X + \text{tense} \begin{bmatrix} \text{Aux}^1 \text{ (not)} \\ \text{be (not)} \\ \text{(not) V} \end{bmatrix} Y \Rightarrow \text{tense} \begin{bmatrix} \text{Aux}^1 \text{ (not) } X \\ \text{be (not) } X \\ \text{(not) } X + V \end{bmatrix} Y$$

Not has been included in parentheses to allow for such sentences as Isn't she going with us?

According to our rules, we can have a deep structure like Q not she is going with us. We apply the transformations in the order (1) negative, (2) yes/no, (3) do. By negative we get the intermediate structure Q she isn't going with us. A structure like this that has had one or more transformations applied to it but which still is not a surface structure is called an intermediate structure. Then the yes/no transformation applies to produce the structure Isn't she going with us? Since tense can be attached to be, the do transformation is inapplicable.

Now let us examine the other kind of question, the WH question, as in What is he saying? This surface structure is derived from Q he is saying something, or preferably Q he is saying NP-WH. After the application of the yes/no transformation, we have the intermediate structure Is he saying NP-WH? The WH transformation substitutes the interrogative what for the noun phrase and shifts it to the beginning of the sentence: What is he saying? These processes are illustrated by the following trees. Here is the deep structure:

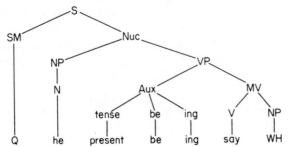

The yes/no transformation applies:

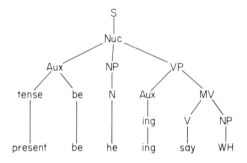

The WH transformation then shifts the NP with **WH** attached to it to the beginning of the sentence and substitutes **what**:

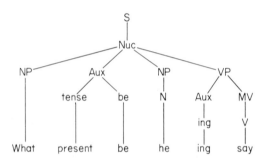

Notice the process in the following sentences. The ones on the left are intermediate structures that have undergone the yes/no transformation; those on the right have had the WH transformation applied to them:

1. are you reading NP-WH              What are you reading?
2. has she torn NP-WH                 What has she torn?
3. were you giving it to NP-WH        Who(m) were you giving it to?

A noun phrase that has **WH** attached to it is replaced by **what** or **who** and moved to the beginning of the sentence.

If the noun phrase with WH-attachment is the object of a preposition, either the whole prepositional phrase or just the noun phrase may be moved. The choice is entirely stylistic, **What are you writing with?** being less formal than **With what are you writing?** We can express this transformation this way:

$$X + \text{(Prep) NP-WH} + Y \Rightarrow \text{(Prep)} \begin{Bmatrix} \text{who} \\ \text{what} \end{Bmatrix} X + Y$$

In the structure are you reading NP-WH now, $X$ is everything before the noun phrase (are you reading) and $Y$ is everything after it (now). Either $X$ or $Y$ may be nothing, as in Are you reading NP-WH, $Y$ is nothing.

As we have stated the rule, there is no way of knowing whether Q you saw NP-WH will become What did you see? or Whom did you see? This choice between who and what depends on whether the NP has the feature [ + human ] or not. The deep structure will attach to the NP not just WH, but also [ + human ] or [ − human ]. The lexicon will give who as [ + human ] and what as [ − human ].

But noun phrases are not the only structures that may have WH attachment. We may find it on an adverbial of place, as in Where are you going? which derives from are you going Adv-p-WH. Various adverbials may have WH attachment; the interrogatives that replace them are listed below, along with a possible answer:

| Adverbial | Replacement | Answer |
|---|---|---|
| place (Adv-p) | where | there; in the yard |
| time (Adv-t) | when | then; tomorrow |
| manner (Adv-m) | how | carefully; with care |
| reason (Adv-r) | why | because of her; for me |

In addition to noun phrases and adverbials, determiners may have WH attachment. Whose replaces a possessive (my, his, John's, etc.); which (and sometimes what) replaces possessives or demonstratives. The WH transformational rule may be summarized as follows:

$$X \begin{bmatrix} \text{Adv-p-WH} \\ \text{Adv-t-WH} \\ \text{Adv-m-WH} \\ \text{Adv-r-WH} \\ \\ \text{Det-WH} + \text{N} \\ \\ \text{(Prep) NP-WH} \end{bmatrix} Y \Rightarrow \begin{bmatrix} \text{where} \\ \text{when} \\ \text{how} \\ \text{why} \\ \left\{ \begin{array}{l} \text{whose} \\ \text{which} \\ \text{what} \end{array} \right\} + \text{N} \\ \text{(Prep)} \left\{ \begin{array}{l} \text{who} \\ \text{what} \end{array} \right\} \end{bmatrix} X + Y$$

## exercises

A. Transform the following deep structures into surface structures:
1. Q you present be going to the movie
2. Q the student past see the flag
3. Q I present may leave
4. Q you present be afraid
5. Q they past know you

B. Give the deep structure from which each of the following sentences was transformed:
   1. Are you watching the clouds?
   2. Have you eaten today?
   3. Does she know his address?
   4. Were they in the drawer?
   5. Did Bill plant the tree?

C. Our rule for the yes/no transformation changes the deep structure **Q you present have a dime** to **Do you have a dime?** It will not produce **Have you a dime?** Similarly, the negative transformation of **not you present have a dime** produces **You don't have a dime**, but not **You haven't a dime**. **Have you a dime?** and **You haven't a dime** are still common in British English, although they are dying out in American English. Can you revise our rule or add a new one to take care of these structures?

D. Perform the WH and *do* transformations, where applicable, on the following intermediate structures:
   1. were they singing NP-WH
   2. present you live Adv-p-WH
   3. was she answering Adv-m-WH
   4. have they answered Det-WH questions
   5. past you see NP-WH

E. Transform the following deep structures into surface structures, performing the transformations in the order (1) negative, (2) yes/no, (3) WH, (4) *do*, and only one at a time:
   1. Q Bob will speak Adv-p-WH
   2. Q not he is going Adv-r-WH
   3. Q he wrote with NP-WH
   4. Q not you have found Det-WH book
   5. Q she wanted NP-WH

F. Give the deep structure from which this sentence was derived: **What could the man have been doing?**
   1. From the deep structure give the words that are represented by the following: $Aux^1$, V, M, be, Aux, MV, VP.
   2. Which tense is found in this sentence? Which word shows the tense?
   3. In this sentence why is the **ing** form of **do** used instead of **does** or **done**? Why is the **en** form of **be** necessary? (Answer these questions from the standpoint of form, not meaning.)
   4. Perform the yes/no transformation on your deep structure. From the rewrite rule for the WH transformation, which words in this intermediate structure are represented by $X$? by $Y$?

G. Why do modals not have **en** or **ing** forms?

H. In the yes/no rule for sentences containing auxiliaries, why do we specify $Aux^1$ instead of just **Aux**?

I. The verb **have** has an **ing** form (**having**), but the auxiliary **have** does not. Why?

# chapter seven
## TRANSFORMATIONAL
## PROCESSES

We have seen that the phrase structure section of a transformational grammar enables us to produce a limited number of simple structures such as the following:

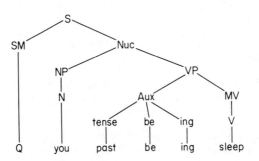

We call this an underlying or **deep** structure. Since this structure contains the SM Q, it meets the conditions for the yes/no transformation, which rearranges the structure:

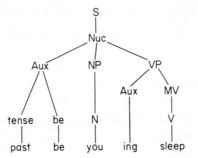

Since this structure does not contain **not** or WH, it does not meet the conditions for the other transformations we have discussed so far. This is, then, a surface structure. The rules in the phonological component of the grammar will give the structure a pronounceable form: **Were you sleeping?**

A transformation may involve any of four processes: addition, deletion, rearrangement, or substitution.

1. By *addition* we place something in the tree that was not in the deep structure; thus, we may add **do** to

   he past not disappear

   to give:

   he past do not disappear

   Since the deep structure must contain the full meaning of the sentence, only words which are relatively empty in meaning, such as **do**, may be added transformationally.

2. By *deletion* we remove something from the structure. We have not yet encountered deletion, but you can readily see how it operates on the following structure:

   Bill couldn't hear you, but I could hear you.
   Bill couldn't hear you, but I could.

   In the second sentence the MV underlying **hear you** has been deleted, since it is repetitious. Only elements that cause no loss in meaning may be deleted.

3. *Rearrangement* changes the ordering of the structure. We have seen this process in the negative, yes/no, and WH transformations. As with the other transformations, rearrangement produces a change in structure and is not just a shifting of words.

4. *Substitution* involves replacing an element of the deep structure with another element, as the substitution of **where** for *Adv-p-WH*. The WH transformation involves a combination of rearrangement and substitution.

In this chapter we will examine several transformations that illustrate these four processes.


## ADVERBIAL MOVEMENT

Our phrase-structure rules introduce all adverbials after the MV, as in sentences 1a, 2a, and 3a:

1a. I saw her at the bank **yesterday.**

2a. He found some luggage in the closet.

3a. We didn't stay long because of the rain.

The following are also grammatical sentences of English:

1b. Yesterday I saw her at the bank.

2b. In the closet he found some luggage.

3b. Because of the rain we didn't stay long.

Since these sentences mean the same thing as the corresponding sentences 1a, 2a, and 3a, we would like to account for this in our grammar. The structure underlying I saw her at the bank yesterday is as follows:

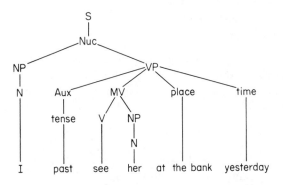

It will be possible to derive Yesterday I saw her at the bank from this same deep structure if we rearrange the elements:

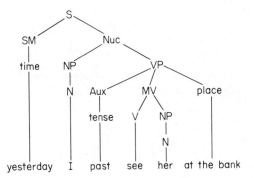

Many adverbials may undergo this rearrangement:

1a. I eat there sometimes.
  b. Sometimes I eat there.

2a. I read about the accident in the newspaper.
  b. In the newspaper I read about the accident.

Most adverbials of manner do not shift except for emphasis: *Carefully he checked the papers. The adverbial-movement transformation, like the negative and yes/no, rearranges the structure underlying a sentence.

## INDIRECT OBJECTS

Now let us turn to another group of sentences which share meaning:

1a. They sent a note to me.
 b. They sent me a note.
2a. Mary has mailed a letter to her friend.
 b. Mary has mailed her friend a letter.
3a. She cooked a meal for me.
 b. She cooked me a meal.

Our phrase-structure rules will account for 1a, 2a, and 3a, but not for 1b, 2b, and 3b, in which the words me (1b), her friend (2b), and me (3b) are said to function as indirect objects. Since sentences 1a and 1b mean the same thing, we would like to derive them from the same deep structure:

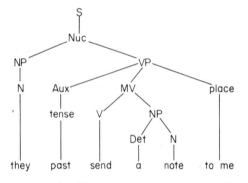

This is the deep structure for **They sent a note to me.** If we rearrange the structure, we can derive sentence 1b:

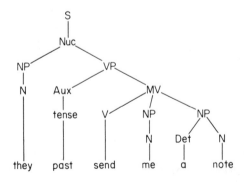

This transformation rearranges; it also deletes the preposition **to**.

It is not enough to say that a transformation rearranges a structure. We must know what kind of structure the transformation may be applied to. For example, the negative transformation applies only to those deep, structures containing the SM **not**, the yes/no only to those containing **Q**. Also, we must know specifically how the structure is rearranged. We write a rule in which the left side defines the structure to which the transformation is to be applied and in which the right side describes the structure after the change is made. In our other rules we included an element to trigger the transformation: **not**, **WH**, **Q**. These transformations are different from the indirect object transformation. In the others, the transformed sentence has a different meaning from the related untransformed sentence without **not**, **Q**, etc. **She was going to town**, a sentence without the optional SM **not**, does not mean the same thing as **She was not going to town**, in which **not** has been selected. But look at the sentences involving indirect objects. **They sent a note to me** and **They sent me a note** are exact paraphrases of each other. The indirect object transformation is optional; there is, therefore, no marker in the deep structure to indicate that it must be performed. We might state our rule as follows:

$$X + V + NP^1 + \begin{Bmatrix} to \\ for \end{Bmatrix} + NP^2 \Rightarrow X + V + NP^2 + NP^1$$

The NPs are numbered so that we can distinguish them. We may illustrate the sentence **She cooked a meal for me** as follows:

| $X$ | $V$ | $NP^1$ | for | $NP^2 \Rightarrow$ | $X$ | $V$ | $NP^2$ | $NP^1$ |
|---|---|---|---|---|---|---|---|---|
| she past | cook | a meal | for | me $\Rightarrow$ | she past | cook | me | a meal |

We want to state our rules precisely enough so that they will permit all grammatical sentences of English; at the same time, we want to prevent all ungrammatical ones. This rule will account for **They sent me a note** and the other sentences we have given, but it will also permit the following:

1. *They sent me it.
2. *Mary has mailed her friend it.
3. *The driver must have given John it.

From these sentences we see that in the deep structure the first NP following the verb must contain a common noun, but the NP after the preposition may contain any kind of nominal. Hence, the structure of **They sent the book to me** fulfills this requirement since **book** is a common noun. **They sent it to me** does not since **it** is not a common noun. We are speaking only of American English, since there are slight differences found in British usage. We should now revise the rule:

$$X + V + (\text{Det}) \begin{bmatrix} + \text{N} \\ + \text{common} \end{bmatrix} + \begin{Bmatrix} \text{to} \\ \text{for} \end{Bmatrix} + \text{NP} \Rightarrow$$

$$X + V + \text{NP} + (\text{Det}) \begin{bmatrix} + \text{N} \\ + \text{common} \end{bmatrix}$$

This rule is optional. Whether we apply it or not depends upon stylistic preferences. It will transform **We shipped the fruit to Tom** to **We shipped Tom the fruit** and **We made a bird house for Sam** to **We made Sam a bird house.** In American English it will not apply to **They gave it to me** or **We threw it to John.**


## IMPERATIVES


Now that we have examined several transformations involving rearrangement, let us look at one of the other processes. An imperative sentence such as **Close the door** or **Be good** has obviously undergone a transformation, since there is no noun phrase before the verb. This NP must have been deleted. Traditional grammarians said that these sentences are derived from **You close the door** and **You be good.** At first glance, **You close the door** appears to pose no problem, but the string *you +  tense + be + good* yields **You are good** or **You were good,** not **You be good.** If we inquire about tense in **You close the door,** we see that this cannot be turned into past tense and retain the same meaning. The traditional explanation is not valid.

We may gain insight into what deep structures underlie **Close the door** and **Be good** by examining tag questions like the following:

1. He was ready, wasn't he?
2. They had been sleeping, hadn't they?
3. You can ski, can't you?
4. She had finished the book, hadn't she?
5. You will go, won't you?

The first part of these sentences before the comma is generated by the phrase-structure rules that we have already outlined. Following the comma is a repetition of tense, $\text{Aux}^1$, and noun phrase. We could write a rule for this kind of tag question:

$$\text{NP} + \text{tense} + \text{Aux}^1 + X \Rightarrow \text{NP} + \text{tense} + \text{Aux}^1 + X + \text{tense}$$

$$+ \text{Aux}^1 + \text{not} + \text{NP}$$

Notice that the tense remains the same, that the first occurring auxiliary is repeated, and that there is no change in the noun phrase: He was going, wasn't he? but not *He was going, isn't she?

Now let us see what tag questions are necessary for imperatives:

1. Close the door, won't you?

2. Be good, won't you?

3. Answer my question, won't you?

These examples show that in the deep structure the noun phrase is you, the tense is present, and the first auxiliary is will. These three sentences must go back to structures similar to You will close the door, You will be good, and You will answer my question. These structures have no morpheme in them that requires a transformation; we, therefore, add the sentence modifier **Imp** (imperative). We now can generate a deep structure like this: Imp you present will go home. Notice that this differs from the deep structure of you will go home by the inclusion of Imp, which means that the sentence is an imperative.

Here is the rule for the imperative transformation:

$$\text{Imp (not)} + \text{you} + \text{present} + \text{will} + X \Rightarrow \text{(not)} \ X$$

This rule is an example of the process of **deletion**. Notice that it is much more restrictive than the others we have encountered. In the other transformations we were able to use NP, since they apply for all kinds of noun phrases in the same way. The imperative transformation, on the other hand, applies only to sentences containing you as the first noun phrase. One principle of our grammar is that the listener must always be able to understand unambiguously which words are deleted. If just any NP were deleted, he would not be able to do this; but if there is a rule saying that you in imperatives may be deleted, both speaker and listener have no problem deciding what has been left out. Similarly, we must specify present tense, not just tense, since sentences with past tense cannot undergo this transformation. Finally, the first auxiliary must be will, not just any modal. When you hear someone say Open the door or Be on time, you are able to recover the deleted information unambiguously. Deleted information is always understood by both speaker and listener.

We have now examined in some detail the four transformational processes: rearrangement, substitution, addition, and deletion. All transformations involve one or more of these processes in converting deep structures into intermediate or surface structures. Transformations alter the structure of the sentence, but they do not affect the meaning given by the deep structure.

## exercises

A. Perform the indirect object transformation:
   1. She has mailed a letter to me.
   2. The farmer gave a watermelon to Fred.
   3. Those people threw pennies to the dancer.
   4. Someone was telling a story to us.
   5. Don must have handed the eraser to Bill.
B. Transform the following deep structures into surface structures. Take the transformations one at a time and in the order (1) imperative, (2) negative, (3) yes/no, (4) WH, (5) *do*.
   1. Imp you will wash the car now
   2. Imp not you will open a window
   3. Q he can do NP-WH
   4. Imp you will tell the answer
   5. Q not she arrived on time
C. For each of the following sentences give the deep structure and take it through the relevant transformations to derive the given surface structure:
   1. He didn't tell me his plans.
   2. Where are you singing tonight?
   3. Listen to me.
   4. Yesterday he didn't know her address.
   5. Why aren't you ready?

# chapter eight
## *THE PASSIVE*
## *TRANSFORMATION*

Because transformations affect form, two surface structures may be different but share the same deep structure. On the surface, **She read me a story** and **She read a story to me** are different, but the native speaker of English understands them to mean the same thing. Our grammar shows how the sentences are related by saying that they have the same deep structure but that the optional indirect object transformation has been applied to the structure of the first sentence but not to that of the second. Here are some more pairs of sentences that share meaning:

1a. Walter saw me.
  b. I was seen by Walter.
2a. The boys had eaten the cake.
  b. The cake had been eaten by the boys.
3a. The waiter is clearing the table.
  b. The table is being cleared by the waiter.

In each of these pairs of sentences the two noun phrases have been interchanged:

| Walter | saw | me |
| I | was seen | by Walter |

In addition, the auxiliary has been expanded. This expansion of the auxiliary should be examined carefully. Below only the sequence **Aux + V** has been given:

1. past              + see            saw
 past + be + en + see          was seen
2. past + have + en         + eat    had eaten
 past + have + en + be + en + eat   had been eaten
3. present + be + ing        + clear   is clearing
 present + be + ing + be + en + clear   is being cleared

It should be obvious now that *be* + *en* has been added between the auxiliary and the verb.

You remember that en is the abbreviation for "past participle of." We earlier saw this form after the auxiliary have: have seen, have eaten, have torn, have slammed, have opened, have set, have hit. In passive sentences the same past participle occurs, but it follows a form of be: was seen, was eaten, was torn, was slammed, was opened, was set, was hit.

We may state the passive rule as follows:

$$(\text{SM}) \; \text{NP}^1 + \text{Aux} + \text{V} + \text{NP}^2 + X \Rightarrow (\text{SM}) \; \text{NP}^2 + \text{Aux} + \text{be}$$
$$+ \text{en} + \text{V} + \text{by} + \text{NP}^1 + X$$

Both **Walter saw me** and **I was seen by Walter** have the following deep structure:

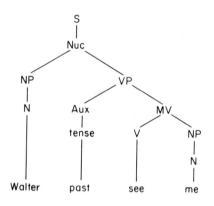

Since the passive transformation is optional, we may skip it and go directly to the phonological rules, giving the sentence **Walter saw me**. But if we apply the passive transformation, we obtain the following derived structure:

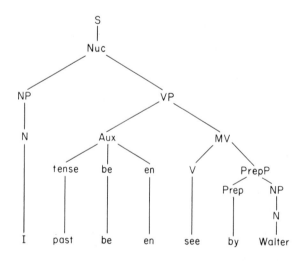

Phonological rules will turn this into **I was seen by Walter**.

There is no difference in meaning between passive sentences and their corresponding actives. This transformation, like the one that produces indirect objects, makes stylistic variations but not changes in meaning. The passive is often less direct than the active and serves a useful function when a person wants to emphasize the object or when the actor is unimportant or unknown:

1. My house was destroyed by the storm.
2. I've been stung.
3. He was wounded in battle.

Not all verbs that have noun phrases following them may undergo the passive transformation:

1. Bill has a cold. *A cold is had by Bill.
2. The book cost a dollar. *A dollar was cost by the book.
3. The box contained a secret.
4. That dress suits her personality perfectly.
5. She resembles her mother slightly.
6. He married his childhood sweetheart.
7. The room measures twelve feet across.

There is one sentence in which **have** occurs in the passive: **A good time was had by all.** This is, of course, an exception. There are also two exceptional verbs that have passives but no corresponding actives: **to be born** and **to be had** ("to be taken advantage of"). For some of these verbs, such as **have**, there will be a feature listed in the lexical entries to block the passive transformation. Others can probably be shown to result from deep structures in which there is no NP after the verb.

Sometimes the deep structure subject is vague, as in these sentences:

1a. Someone signed the paper.
2a. Someone has found the car.
3a. Something stung me.

By the passive transformation these can become

1b. The paper was signed by someone.
2b. The car has been found by someone.
3b. I was stung by something.

We may apply the *deletion transformation* to the prepositional phrase containing the indefinite someone or something:

1c. The paper was signed.
2c. The car has been found.
3c. I was stung.

Only indefinites or other obvious NPs, such as The defendant was found guilty (by the jury) may be deleted. The listener must always be able to understand what has been deleted.

It is possible with the selection or rejection of various optional transformations to have several different surface structures all deriving from the same deep structure:

1. Deep structure:          Someone past hand a note to Fred
   Surface structure:       Someone handed a note to Fred.
2. Deep structure:          Someone past hand a note to Fred
   T-indirect object:       Someone past hand Fred a note
   Surface structure:       Someone handed Fred a note.
3. Deep structure:          Someone past hand a note to Fred
   T-passive:               A note past be en hand to Fred by someone
   Surface structure:       A note was handed to Fred by someone.
4. Deep structure:          Someone past hand a note to Fred
   T-passive:               A note past be en hand to Fred by someone
   T-deletion:              A note past be en hand to Fred
   Surface structure:       A note was handed to Fred.
5. Deep structure:          Someone past hand a note to Fred
   T-indirect object:       Someone past hand Fred a note
   T-passive:               Fred past be en hand a note by someone
   Surface structure:       Fred was handed a note by someone.
6. Deep structure:          Someone past hand a note to Fred
   T-indirect object:       Someone past hand Fred a note
   T-passive:               Fred past be en hand a note by someone
   T-deletion:              Fred past be en hand a note
   Surface structure:       Fred was handed a note.

The native speaker recognizes all six sentences as meaning the same thing. Our grammar accounts for this.

Grammarians in the past were often concerned with the meaning of the terms *subject of* and *object of*. In the sentence Her husband washed the dishes, there is no problem. Her husband, the actor, is in subject position before the verb; the dishes, the receiver, is in object position after the verb.

A passive, however, such as **The dishes were washed by her husband,** presents a problem, since the actor is not in subject position nor the receiver in object position. Some grammarians spoke of **the dishes** as being the grammatical subject but logical object. In transformational grammar there is no problem. Such functions as subject and object have meaning only at a specific level, and these functions do not necessarily correspond among levels. Hence, in the deep structure **her husband** is the subject and **the dishes** is the object. In the surface structure, however, **the dishes** is the subject and **her husband** the object of a preposition. Since meaning is reflected in the deep structure and form in the surface structure, there is no problem of "logical subject" and "grammatical subject."

Our grammar also accounts for certain feature restrictions. In Chapter Four we saw that the following sentences are ungrammatical because they violate feature restrictions:

1a.  *Honesty admired the man.

2a.  *Sue amazed his honesty.

The corresponding passives are also ungrammatical:

1b.  *The man was admired by honesty.

2b.  *His honesty was amazed by Sue.

If we were limited to surface structures in explaining feature restrictions, we could not merely say that **honesty** may not be a subject of **admire,** for the sentence **Honesty is admired by the man** is perfectly grammatical. One rule based solely on surface structures would have to contain the following points:

1.  **Admire** may not have an abstract subject in active sentences: *Honesty admired the man.

2.  **Admire** may have an abstract subject in passive sentences: Honesty is admired by the man.

3.  In passive sentences abstract nouns may not occur in **by** phrases following **admire:** *The man is admired by honesty.

Such a statement of facts, although true, has two serious weaknesses: it is uneconomical in wording, and it fails to show that the three points have something in common. Yet the native speaker feels that there is some relationship among the three points, that it is precisely the fact that *Honesty admired the man is ungrammatical which makes *The man was admired by honesty ungrammatical. A grammar that recognizes deep structure can both shorten the rule and, more importantly, show the relationships among the parts: "Admire may not have a deep structure subject that is abstract; it has no restrictions on the deep structure object." Hence, neither *Honesty admired the man nor *The man was admired by honesty will be possible since they would share the same deep structure which has been blocked by the feature constraints. Both The man admired honesty and Honesty was admired by the man are possible, since their common deep structure violates no constraints.

## exercises

A. Perform the passive transformation on the following structures:
   1. The maid was sweeping the floor.
   2. Jane sang a song in the theater.
   3. Tom must have milked the cow yesterday.
   4. The man was throwing the pillow.
   5. The sailor could have sunk the boat.

B. Write the deep structure from which each of the following sentences was derived:
   1. The rocks are being hurled by that boy.
   2. Treasure was found by the pirate.
   3. The note could have been planted by the suspect.
   4. John was being persuaded by them.
   5. Your lesson could be prepared by Sam.

C. Below are five pairs of surface structures that differ. In each pair if the sentences mean the same thing, account for their differences in form by giving their deep structure and showing which transformations have been applied. If the two sentences do not mean the same thing, show how their deep structures account for this:
   1a. Sally has been sent a present.
    b. Someone has sent a present to Sally.
   2a. What has he discovered in the drawer?
    b. Has he discovered something in the drawer?
   3a. Didn't he tell the secret to his wife?
    b. Didn't he tell his wife the secret?
   4a. Bill wasn't fired by the superintendent.
    b. The superintendent didn't fire Bill.
   5a. You won't be staying there long.
    b. Don't stay there long.

part three

*TRANSFORMATIONS I I*

# chapter nine

## PRINCIPLES OF TRANSFORMATIONAL GRAMMAR

Now that we have discussed the phrase structure, the lexical features, and the process of transformation, you are in a better position to understand the principles of transformational grammar than when we first mentioned them in Chapter One. It will be useful now for us to restate those principles and illustrate them with material from the grammar that you have studied.

During the first years of a child's life, he hears many sentences spoken. Eventually he begins experimenting with sentences as he tries to speak. He learns to associate objects and actions with specific words, and he learns to combine these words with one another to produce larger, meaningful structures. The English-speaking child learns that determiners precede nouns and that prepositions precede noun phrases. He learns that if he has more than one book, he speaks of his **books**; similarly, the plural of **toy** is **toys** and of **dish** is **dishes**. The plural ending is pronounced differently in each of these words. When he learns a new noun, he automatically applies his rule for plural formation to it and produces **cats, ducks, dogs, foots,** and **mans.** The last two he later learns are exceptions and memorizes their plurals. When the child says **foots** or **mans,** we know that he has mastered the rule for plural formation in English. By the time he is five or six, he has mastered many other rules, such as word order and past-tense formation. We do not know what form these rules have taken in his mind, since their application becomes routine with him. The rules he has developed which permit him to understand and produce the sentences of his language are collectively known as a *grammar.* The child's grammar constitutes his knowledge of the language.

Each person develops a grammar of his language. Furthermore, he develops it largely by himself with very little technical help except an occasional correction such as "Don't say **singed**; say **sang.**" It should not be surprising, then, that no two people develop exactly the same grammar. People's speech patterns are as distinctive as their fingerprints. This uniqueness is made obvious by our ability to recognize many people's voices

75

on the telephone, radio, or television. Less obvious but no less distinctive are the choices people make in selecting words and syntactic patterns.

Although each person develops his own unique grammar, it has much in common with the grammars developed by other people with whom he comes in contact; otherwise, they would not be able to communicate with him or would think he sounded odd. In fact, most English-speaking people can understand one another. As we might expect, a person's grammar will be quite similar to those of the people he is in frequent contact with. He will sound more like people in his own family than people in another part of town, more like people from his own region of the country than people from other regions, more like people from his own social class than people from other classes.

We refer to an expression as *grammatical* for this person if it conforms to the rules of the grammar that he has developed. When his rules are the same as the rules of other speakers of his language, all will agree that certain expressions are grammatical and others ungrammatical. The following are ungrammatical for all speakers of English:

1. *Book the on the table is.
2. *The girl seemed.
3. *The man elapsed.

Other structures are grammatical for some speakers but not for others:

1. She looked a fool.
2. We shan't be long.
3. We might should do it.
4. We seen it.
5. We have saw it.
6. We have seen it.

For the speaker of sentence 4, the principal parts of see are probably see, seen, seen; for the speaker of sentence 5, see, saw, saw; for the speaker of sentence 6, see, saw, seen. These differences exist because these three speakers probably were not in contact with the same people as they were learning to talk. Each one developed a rule based on the raw material that he heard. Notice that the grammars which produced sentences 4 and 5 have only two distinct principal parts for see; the grammar that produced sentence 6 has probably made a similar simplification for such verbs as cling, slink, stink, and shrink, all of which originally had three distinct forms. Each of the above six sentences is grammatical for some speakers of

English; none is grammatical for all. Notice that our use of *grammatical* means nothing more than that the structure under consideration follows the rules of whatever grammar we are discussing. We are not using this term to appraise the grammar for its effectiveness or its ability to conceal one's regional or social origin.

The rules comprising this grammar that each person creates are limited in number; also, the number of words each person uses and understands is finite. With a limited number of words and rules for combining them into larger structures, a person is able to create and to understand an *infinite* number of sentences. You would see that this statement is not exaggerated if you looked for repetitions of sentences in a large book. And if you taped your own conversations for a week, you would find that such repeated structures as **Good morning, How are you?** and **What time is it?** make up a very small part of what you say; there is very little repetition in your other sentences. Although you are not conscious of it, most of the sentences you encounter each day are totally new to you; on the other hand, the rules that formed these sentences are very well known to you. This is one of the ways your speech differs from that of a talking bird. The bird says only sentences it has memorized. You have memorized almost no sentences, and it would be impossible for you to memorize all of the ones you need or can use. You are able to make use of a finite set of elements and rules to create an infinite number of sentences.

If there were some way to discover the form these rules assume in a person's mind, the linguist's task of describing the language would be easy. As it is, he must be content with trying to describe the regular patterns that he observes. His description is expressed in the form of rules, and we call his collection of rules a *grammar*. We, therefore, use *grammar* with two meanings. The first is the rules a person has developed which permit him to understand and to create sentences in his language. The second is a theory about these rules and is an artificial, less efficient way of expressing them. It tries to describe the native speaker's knowledge of his language; no one claims that it succeeds in duplicating this knowledge, nor is it likely that it ever will. *Subject, object, noun phrase,* etc. are terms the linguist has created to describe certain relations. Although the *concepts* that these terms name must exist in the individual's grammar, the terms belong strictly to the grammar of the linguist. We avoid further confusion over the word *grammar* by referring to such matters as choice between **don't** and **doesn't, who** and **whom** as **usage**. Notice that this kind of grammar is intended not as a model for learning one's language. Such a grammar attempts the much more difficult task of describing the grammar that the individual has developed.

The central component of transformational grammars is **syntax**, which consists of two divisions: the phrase structure and the transformations.

The phrase structure generates abstract deep structures such as

SM + Det + N + past + be + ing + V + N + Pl

and it also gives a structural description to this string of elements, telling us that Det + N is a noun phrase, that past + be + ing is an auxiliary, etc. The elements N and V are assigned features (+ common, + human, + ___ NP, etc.) which are then matched with entries in a lexicon to give the following:

Q + the + woman + past + be + ing + sell + apple + Pl

With this string and its structural description we momentarily leave the syntactic component.

The second division of the grammar is the **semantic** component, which operates on the deep structure. The morpheme Q contains the meaning of "question" in the deep structure of the above sentence and gives it a different meaning from the related positive statement, in which Q has not been selected. The semantic component shows how the meanings of the lexical items combine to give the meaning of the sentence as determined by the syntactic structure. As an example of the dependence of the semantic component upon syntax, look at the following group of words: old several buckets rusty metal. Unless you rearrange the words in your mind, you see no meaning beyond that of each word in isolation. If you rearrange the words to read several old rusty metal buckets, you find more meaning than is contained in the individual words. You are able to apply the rules in the semantic component because you perceive a syntactic structure.

We now return to the syntactic component and apply transformational rules to our structure to produce

past + be + the + woman + ing + sell + apple + Pl

This transformation has rearranged elements, but it has not affected the meaning. Other transformations may add or delete elements; some substitute one element for another.

The third division is the **phonological** component. It tells us, among other things, to pronounce past + be as was or were, ing + sell as selling, and apple + pl as apples. It gives us an intonation pattern that differs from that of a group of words read as a list. The phonological component operates on the surface structure and gives the sentence its final form. We will describe the phonological component in Part Four of this text.

Transformationalists hope that their grammars will eventually specify all of the grammatical sentences of the language and no ungrammatical ones;

this is the proficiency that a native speaker has. No such grammar has yet been written.

Earlier, structural linguists felt that the ideal way to collect data for their observations about language was to gather large samples of speech, preferably recorded without the speaker's knowledge, and to analyze them. The transformationalists argue that if the linguist does nothing more than analyze such a corpus of material he is studying the speaker's **performance** of his language, rather than his **competence**. If a speaker changes his train of thought in the middle of a sentence, this structure will be analyzed along with the "normal" ones, as will false starts and words that are out of place. Furthermore, the corpus may lack certain constructions, such as passives or indirect objects. The structural approach analyzes only observed utterances and makes no comments about those that are not observed. The transformational approach, however, is as concerned with potential utterances as it is with those actually spoken at a given time. It attempts to state whether a structure that has not actually been observed is possible or not. The transformationalist is interested in the speaker's competence, the grammar that he has developed. He has to study the speaker's performance, or application of the grammar, but it is merely as a means of approaching the underlying system. In addition, he makes use of the speaker's comments about his language, while realizing that these comments may be inaccurate.

We can see the difference between competence and performance if we look at an example. In speaking about competence, we will use the terms *grammatical* and *ungrammatical*; for performance we will use *acceptable* and *unacceptable*. In a moment of excitement a person might scream, House is on fire! If we are speaking of performance, the sentence is acceptable; it will communicate the idea perfectly well and get the desired results. From the standpoint of competence, the sentence is ungrammatical: house is a singular count noun and may not exist without a determiner. Studying the sentence will add nothing to our understanding of the underlying system of English determiners; in fact, it could easily lead to the false generalization that determiners which are normally obligatory are omitted in certain circumstances. We would be basing this assertion on only one sentence, and we would have a long wait before we heard another spontaneous utterance like it. On the other hand, if we ask a native speaker about House is on fire! he will confirm our original impression that this is a nonce occurrence. It is also possible for a structure to be grammatical but unacceptable because it is too long, too conversational, too formal, etc.

The transformationalist in studying the system of language says that every sentence has a deep structure and a surface structure. Traditional grammarians at times made similar statements when they said that Go home comes from You go home; that There is a man at the door should be converted from its "inverted order" to its "natural order," A man is at the

**door,** before it can be analyzed, that **He is as tall as John** comes from **He is as tall as John is tall,** etc. Unfortunately, the traditional grammars that have been the most popular during the last two hundred years made no systematic use of this concept.

The distinction between deep and surface structure gives us much insight into the structure of sentences. Most people probably more or less convert a sentence to its deep structure when they point out the subjects and objects in the following sentences:

1. There is too much noise in the room.
2. There were some people leaning against the wall.
3. Were you driving the car?
4. What has she done with the screen?
5. The man you saw was he.
6. There's a girl in my class taller than Mary.

At times the surface structure greatly obscures relationships. On the surface, these two sentences look alike:

1. I found the room mentioned by the students.
2. I found the room cluttered by the students.

The second sentence can mean **I found the room cluttered up by the presence of many students,** but usually it means **I found the room messy.** Although the first sentence can also have two parallel meanings, the more usual is **I found the room that the students had mentioned.** The differences lie not so much in semantics as in the arrangement of the deep structure. **Cluttered by the students** can be a reduced relative clause, but in sentence 2, it would usually be an objective complement. It is only through an analysis of underlying or deep structures that this difference can be brought out.

Without the use of deep structure, it is impossible to show the relationship between the following sentences:

1. I looked the number up.
2. I looked up the number.

With deep structure we can show that these sentences originated from a common source; without it, we need two sets of rules for adverbial particles immediately after the verb and at the end of the sentence.

Or look at these sentences:

1. The smiling girl sat down.
2. The charming girl sat down.

Without using deep structure, a person has no way of showing that smiling is a present participle but that charming is an adjective. Nor is there any formal difference in the structures The girl was smiling and The girl was charming. We can account for this difference if we can show that charming is derived transformationally from the deep structure The girl charms people.

Deep structure is a subject that is currently undergoing much discussion and investigation. Many linguists believe that all languages share the same deep structure and that it is much more abstract than any published account has yet indicated. Since humans are all very much alike physically, it does seem reasonable that there are biologically determined universals in language. For example, the tongue is shaped for all people so that the tip cannot be in the front and the back of the mouth at the same time. Research in deep structures of various languages is giving linguists material for comparison and is rapidly adding support for language universals.

People in all cultures of the world have speech, yet no one is ever really taught to talk. The human child hears people speaking and learns to talk largely on his own. Some animals hear as much speech as the human child does, and some of them are given far more attention; yet only the human learns to talk, although some pets have the physical capacity for speech. It is true that some birds learn to repeat a few memorized phrases, but only man learns to create new sentences and to communicate his ideas with speech. Man's brain gives him an aptitude for speech that is lacking in other animals.

As the child is listening to people talk, he hears many mistakes (false starts, stammers, words out of order, etc.) mixed in with "normal" utterances. Occasionally these mistakes are corrected, but usually they are not marked as being different from other utterances. In other words, children encounter only performance, yet all of them develop competence from this exposure to language, even though conditions are usually poor. They learn to create and to understand new sentences, no small accomplishment when we realize how complex human languages are. It seems almost certain that each child has some innate ability for working with the raw language materials he finds in his environment and for developing them into his grammar. The child must bring something more than a blank slate to his language learning. The systematic study of child language learning has only begun, but it will no doubt shed much light on our understanding of our language as more research is performed.

## exercises

A. **Reserved** is an adjective in **Those are reserved men** but a past participle in **Those are reserved seats.** Is this difference entirely semantic, or can you use deep structure to account for it?

B. What is a grammar? What is it intended to provide an account of?

C. It has been said that every normal six-year old knows a grammar of his mother tongue. Explain. How does this meaning of **grammar** differ from that used in question B?

D. Does **grammatical** mean the same thing to the transformationalist as it does to the traditionalist? Explain. Do they both mean the same thing by **rule**?

E. What are some of the objections linguists have to traditional grammar?

F. What is the purpose of studying the grammar of a language?

G. What effect should our understanding of a child's competence in his language have on the teaching of reading in the first few grades?

H. Considering the scope of grammar, how useful do you think is much repetition of words in first-grade readers of the type "Look! Look! Look! See Jack run! Run! Run! Run!" What reactions do you have to the syntax in sentences like these?

# chapter ten
# *COMPOUNDING, DELETION, AND PRO FORMS*

So far we have discussed sentences that derive from only one S. It is possible to join two sentences with a co-ordinating conjunction (and, or, nor, but, yet, for) to produce a compound sentence: Alice wrapped the package, and Susan addressed the card.

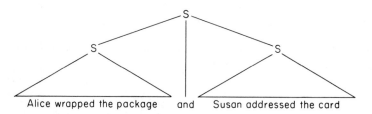

We will restrict the term *compound sentence* to two sentences joined by a co-ordinating conjunction. Other pairs of sentences that may be joined by a semicolon will be treated as two separate sentences: We listened attentively to the entire speech; we did not, however, agree with what he said. Our reason for making this distinction is that two sentences joined by a conjunction may have deletion of identical elements, whereas those without a conjunction may not.

1. We went to the exhibition, but (we) did not stay long. (Deletion of the second **we** is possible.)
2. We went to the exhibition; however, we did not stay long. (No deletion is possible.)

To account for sentences joined together in this fashion, we need to revise our phrase-structure rule for the sentence.

$$P1: S \rightarrow \begin{Bmatrix} S^n \\ (SM) \ Nuc \end{Bmatrix}$$

With this revision we may still select (SM) Nuc as the rewrite for S and generate the sentences we have discussed in the preceding chapters. But we now have another possibility: S may be rewritten as two or more Ss without limit ($S^n$). In the preceding paragraph we saw a sentence in which only two instances of S were selected. It would be possible to extend this indefinitely: **Alice wrapped the package, and Susan addressed the cards, and Beth bought the stamps, and Frances mailed the package.** . . . Such a sentence would be monotonous and stylistically awkward; if we made it very long, no one would be able to remember it all. But these factors do not affect grammaticalness. Because of this rule it is impossible for us to point to any sentence and say that it is the longest in the language. Any sentence can always have another S joined to it.

Our revised rule for S will permit trees such as the following:

A rule will add a conjunction, such as **and**, before each S except the first one:

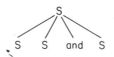

If there are three or more Ss, a further rule will optionally delete all conjunctions except the last one:

The sentences are accounted for by the phrase-structure and transformational rules. Conjunctions are added and deleted by the *conjunction addition* and *deletion* transformations.

There are certain constraints on the compound sentence that we will not be able to explain satisfactorily until more research is performed on how sentences interact with one another. The semantic component, for example, in some way will have to require similarity of meaning: **We like Mozart, but we find Hindemith a bore;** *We like Mozart, but that chair looks** comfortable. The syntactic component will block certain transformations in compound sentences: *I didn't know you had read Beth's letter, and tell me what she said. Normally if one sentence is a question or an imperative, the other must be also if they are joined by and. This restriction does not always hold with but: I have already heard the story, but tell it anyway. The grammar internalized by the native speaker handles these constraints with ease; we hope that transformational grammar will eventually be able to state them precisely.

When identical words occur in both parts of a compound sentence, they are often deleted in one of the sentences:

1. Dave went to the carnival and (Dave) rode the Ferris wheel.
2. Bill sold his car and (Bill sold) his motorcycle.
3. Sue (visited us last night) and her husband visited us last night.
4. I was frightened, and Tony was (frightened), too.
5. I enjoyed the concert, but Sally didn't (enjoy the concert).
6. I could see him, and so could Bob (see him).

Elements deleted by transformations are always clearly understood by both speaker and listener. For example, in the sentence I enjoyed the concert, but Sally didn't, any native speaker of English understands that Sally didn't means Sally didn't enjoy the concert, not Sally didn't go to the concert or Sally didn't wash her hands. This understanding is possible because deletion can occur only under conditions that are very precisely specified. We may delete certain repeated elements, as in the sentences in the preceding paragraph, or we may delete vague or otherwise understood NPs, as we have seen earlier:

1. Janice ate (something).
2. The car has been found (by someone).

Deletion, like other transformations, alters syntactic structures:

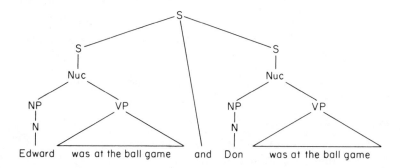

The repeated VP is deleted to give the following derived structure:

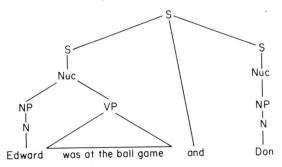

Another transformation will attach the NP **Don** and the conjunction **and** to the first Nuc:

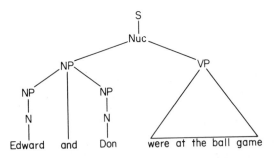

Usually two or more structures may be conjoined if they are alike (i.e., both Ss, both NPs, both VPs, etc.):

1. She is **eager and industrious.** (Two adjectives)
2. They worked **fast but carefully.** (Two adverbials of manner)
3. They **went to bed late** but **got up early.** (Two VPs)

If two different kinds of structure are conjoined, the result is ungrammatical:

1. *She is **friendly** and **a pleasant woman.** (Adjective and NP)
2. *The ball rolled **under the car** and **then.** (Adverbial of place and adverbial of time)

Instead of deleting repeated words, we may substitute a generalized word known as a *Pro form*:

1. **Do** for a VP or a verb
   a. I saw the accident, and Bill **saw the accident,** too.
      I saw the accident, and Bill **did,** too.

b. He won't answer the telephone, but I will **answer** it.
   He won't answer the telephone, but I will **do** it.

2. **There** for an adverbial of place

   We were sitting in the balcony, and they were sitting **in the balcony**, too.
   We were sitting in the balcony, and they were sitting **there**, too.

3. **Then** for an adverbial of time
   He saw Tom yesterday, and we saw Fred **yesterday**, too.
   He saw Tom yesterday, and we saw Fred **then**, too.

4. **One** for a noun or a noun phrase
   a. I have a sister, and you have **a sister**, too.
      I have a sister, and you have **one**, too.
   b. I don't have a new car, but I do have an old **car**.
      I don't have a new car, but I do have an old **one**.

5. **Some, any, every,** and **no** for determiners, added to various Pro forms:
   **someone, anybody, everything, nowhere, sometime,** etc.

6. **He, she, it, they** for NPs
   a. John said that **John** would go with us.
      John said that **he** would go with us.
   b. When I saw Jane, **Jane** looked worried.
      When I saw Jane, **she** looked worried.
   c. I bought a new car and wrecked **a new car** the next day.
      I bought a new car and wrecked **it** the next day.
   d. I don't know the Smiths or **the Smiths'** neighbors.
      I don't know the Smiths or **their** neighbors.

Although we did not label them as such at the time, the WH words which substitute in the WH transformation are Pro forms. The use of Pro forms, especially pronouns, is not restricted to repetition within a sentence: **I didn't know that** *Bill* **lived next door to you. Does** *he* **visit you often?** Some Pro forms, such as **one** and **someone,** are often used because the person they represent is not known or is generalized. We used these forms in explaining the passive transformation when we said that **Someone has found the ring** underlies **The ring has been found.**

   Transformations show how some sentences that are paraphrases of each other are related:

1a. The project was completed by Fred.
 b. Fred completed the project.
2a. Yesterday I found the error.
 b. I found the error yesterday.
3a. Susan received my letter and answered it the same day.
 b. Susan received my letter, and she answered my letter the same day.

4a.  Ann and Susan were discouraged.
  b.  Ann was discouraged, and Susan was discouraged.

It would appear that all conjoined structures—NPs, VPs, adjectives, etc.—are derived from compound sentences.
   Now examine these sentences:

1a.  Bill's paper and Sam's speech were similar.
  b.  *Bill's paper was similar, and Sam's speech was similar.
2a.  He sat between Tom and me.
  b.  *He sat between Tom, and he sat between me.

Certain adjectives, prepositions, and verbs—similar, different, alike, between, to combine, etc.—require compound or plural nouns; hence, the compound sentences 1b and 2b cannot underlie sentences 1a and 2a. There must be a second source for compound NPs. Such a source can be found in an expanded version of the phrase-structure rule for the NP:

$$NP \rightarrow \left\{ \begin{array}{l} (Det)\ N\ (Pl) \\ NP^n \end{array} \right\}$$

This rule is parallel to the one that rewrites S as $S^n$. It produces compound NPs like these:

The same rule that adds conjunctions between compound sentences will do the same thing here:

And a rule will optionally delete all but the last conjunction:

We now have two sources for compound NPs in surface structures:

1. From compound sentences via deletion and rearrangement of structure.
2. From compound NPs in the deep structure.

It is thus possible to have two surface structures identical in form, but derived from different deep structures as shown in the following trees for Ann and Tom are married.

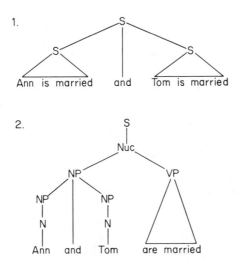

But upon examination we see that this is an ambiguous sentence and that the two meanings correspond to the different derivations.  It can mean:

1. Both Ann and Tom are married. (But not to each other)
2. Ann and Tom are married to each other.

Ann and Tom are married with the meaning of the first paraphrase is derived from the first tree, with the meaning of the second paraphrase from the second tree.  Other examples of ambiguous surface NPs are seen in the following sentences:

1. He drank vodka and orange juice.
2. Bill and Jim earned $200 last week.
3. Mr. Adams and his wife have written several books.

With the meaning of separate actions, paraphrased by structures with both . . . and (He drank both vodka and orange juice), the sentences are derived from compound sentences. With the meaning of a combination, paraphrased by structures with together (He drank vodka and orange juice together), they derive from compound NPs.

    In this chapter we have seen that it is possible to join two or more sentences together; if this conjunction of sentences results in a repetition of words, either the deletion or the Pro-form transformation applies. Some compound NPs are derived through this process, but others are compound in the deep structure.

## exercises

A. For each of the following sentences give the deep structure and show which transformations have been applied:

1. The figurines will remain in the living room, but the flowers will be moved to the den.
2. The Smiths dropped by after work but didn't stay long.
3. I couldn't hear the speech, but Esther could.
4. We went to the lake and to the park.
5. Won't Henry or someone be at home in the morning?
6. He didn't write or telephone us.
7. She is pretty but very dumb.
8. The Smiths left early, and I did, too.
9. Bill arrived early, but he didn't stay long.
10. We were sitting on the front row, and they were sitting there, too.
11. Bach and Handel sound alike to Homer.
12. Susan and Agnes met each other in Seattle.

B. Show how the ambiguity of the following sentences can be accounted for by their deep structures:

1. Herb and Louise got divorced last week.
2. I like hot dogs and ice cream.
3. Patsy and Sam have two children.
4. She invited Pam and Frank.
5. A dog and a cat followed me yesterday.

C. Classify the following sentences as grammatical or ungrammatical and decide what constraints on compounding account for the ungrammatical sentences:

1. The burglar raised the window carefully, and he listened to see whether anyone had heard him, and then he entered the room.
2. He raised the window, but he thought someone might have heard him, but then he entered the room.
3. Why did you quit your job, and when will you find a new one?
4. Why did you leave the door open, and close it.
5. He can sing well, and she can too.
6. He can, and she can sing well too.
7. He can sing well, or she can too.
8. I read this book and that book.
9. I read a book and the book.
10. I heard and saw you enter.
11. I heard or saw you enter.
12. I heard but saw you enter.
13. I didn't know your name, and there's a fly on my nose.
14. He turned in the report, and he turned in his tracks.
15. She is tall but graceful.

# chapter eleven
## RELATIVE CONSTRUCTIONS

The following sentences cannot be accounted for by the rules we have given so far:

a. The boat that he is building is large.

b. Janice picked the flowers which are in the vase.

c. The man whom you met yesterday has painted the garage.

These sentences seem to contain NPs that consist of more elements than Det, N, and Pl; they are not compounds like Jane and Mary. First of all, we should make certain that the italicized elements really are NPs. Here are three kinds of evidence we can use:

1. Pronouns may substitute for them:

a. The boat that he is building is large.
   It is large.

b. Janice picked the flowers which are in the vase.
   Janice picked them.

c. The man whom you met yesterday has painted the garage.
   He has painted the garage.

2. When they occur in subject position, tense and Aux[1] move before them to produce questions:

a. Is the boat that he is building large?

b. Has the man whom you met yesterday painted the garage?

3. Under the passive transformation, they fill the positions of NPs:

   b. **The flowers which are in the vase** were picked by Jane.

   c. The garage has been painted by **the man whom you met yesterday**.

Although additional evidence could readily be found, this is enough to establish the italicized groups of words as NPs.

We can easily break these NPs into three or four elements each:

| Det | N | Pl | unknown element |
|-----|-----|-----|------------------|
| the | boat |  | that he is building |
| the | flower | Pl | which are in the vase |
| the | man |  | whom you met yesterday |

The unknown elements look like transformed sentences with underlying structures like the following:

   a. he is building **the boat**

   b. **the flowers** are in the vase

   c. you met **the man** yesterday

We say that these sentences have been *embedded* into the noun phrases.

The italicized NPs in the deep structure have been moved to the beginning of the embedded sentence by the **relative** transformation:

| | | | |
|---|---|---|---|
| 1. | The boat | he is building **the boat** | is large |
| T-rel | The boat | **the boat** he is building | is large |
| 2. | Jane picked the flowers | **the flowers** are in the vase | |
| T-rel | Jane picked the flowers | **the flowers** are in the vase | |
| 3. | The man | you met **the man** yesterday | has painted the garage |
| T-rel | The man | **the man** you met yesterday | has painted the garage |

If the NP is already at the beginning of the sentence, as in the second example, there is no change in word order; we say, nevertheless, that the relative transformation has been applied.

As we saw in the last chapter, repeated words are normally not permitted in a sentence. We either delete one of them, or we substitute a Pro form for it. Notice how the following structures are transformed by T-rel and T-pro:

1. Deep: The cup    you are washing the cup    is cracked
   T-rel: The cup    the cup you are washing    is cracked
   T-pro: The cup    that you are washing    is cracked

2. Deep: The car    he is riding in the car    is safe
   T-rel: The car    the car he is riding in    is safe
   T-pro: The car    which he is riding in    is safe

We call who, which, and that **relative pronouns** and the clauses they introduce **relative clauses.**

To account for relative clauses, we must expand our rewrite rule for the NP:

$$NP \rightarrow \begin{Bmatrix} (Det)\ N\ (Pl) \\ NP + S \quad \text{— } \text{\tiny rel}. \\ NP^n \end{Bmatrix}$$

In the preceding chapters we have seen many NPs generated by the choices of (Det) N (Pl) and of $NP^n$; here is a diagram illustrating the other choice: The embedded sentence you saw the man will become the relative clause whom you saw, and the entire sentence will be The man whom you saw waved. One constraint placed on this structure is that the embedded sentence must contain an NP identical to the one preceding the sentence, such as the man in

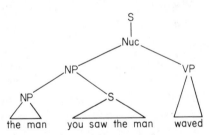

this case. The deep structure The man (you saw the duck) waved cannot be transformed into a grammatical surface structure becuase of this constraint.

If the NP has the feature [ + human ], either who or that may be selected:

1. He is the man who spoke.

2. He is the man that spoke.

3. *He is the man which spoke.

If the NP has the feature [ — human ], either that or which may be selected:

1. This is the house that he bought.
2. This is the house which he bought.
3. *This is the house whom he bought.

If the NP is the object of a preposition, the preposition may be shifted with the NP or not: She is the girl who(m) I danced with; She is the girl with whom I danced. If the preposition is shifted, whom must be used instead of who, and that may not be selected:

1. The chair that I sat in was broken.
2. *The chair in that I sat was broken.
3. The chair in which I sat was broken.
4. She is the girl that I talked to.
5. *She is the girl to that I talked.
6. She is the girl to whom I talked.
7. *She is the girl to who I talked.

The relative pronoun may be derived from any NP in the deep structure:

1. Subject | the girls arrived late
who arrived late

2. Direct object | we saw the girls
whom we saw

3. Object of a preposition | they talked about the cars
about which they talked

4. Subjective complement | she had become a witch
that she had become

5. Objective complement | we called him a name
which we called him

Another kind of introductory word found in relative clauses is the relative adverb:

1. This is the town where I was born.
2. We argued about the time when he left.

These are easily accounted for by our grammar:

1. I was born in the town      where I was born
2. he left at that time        when he left

In Chapter Nine we said that the semantic component assigns a meaning to the deep structure and that transformations do not affect this meaning. Since He gave me a dollar and He gave a dollar to me share the same lexical items (except to) and the two sentences mean the same thing, we expect them to be derived from the same deep structure, as is indeed the case. Now look at this pair of sentences:

1. The man whom you saw looks like Jim.
2. The man you saw looks like Jim.

Since these sentences mean the same thing, they must share a common deep structure: The man you saw the man looks like Jim. By T-rel this becomes The man the man you saw looks like Jim. If we apply T-pro, we get The man whom you saw looks like Jim. In Chapter Ten we saw that there are two possibilities for avoiding repetition: replacement by a Pro form and deletion. Instead of applying T-pro, we may apply T-del and get The man you saw looks like Jim. The difference in the two surface structures results from a different selection of transformations. Here are some more possibilities:

1.  This is the coat (which) I bought.
2.  The boat (that) I found had been abandoned.
3.  I am frightened by the kind of person (that) he has become.
4.  He is the man (whom) we talked with.
5.  He is the man with whom we talked.
6.  *He is the man with we talked.
7.  Students who ask questions learn quickly.
8.  *Students ask questions learn quickly.

As you can see from the last two sentences, if the NP derives from a subject in its deep structure, it may not be deleted; the same restriction applies to an object of a preposition if the preposition is shifted with the NP (sentences 5 and 6). In all other cases the NP is freely deletable. Even with deletion, these are still called relative clauses.

Any time that we have two surface structures with shared vocabulary and the same meaning, we expect them to have the same deep structure.

These two sentences mean the same thing:

1. The woman **who is waiting for John** is his wife.
2. The woman **waiting for John** is his wife.

The second sentence has undergone a different deletion transformation. This optional transformation deletes relative pronoun, tense, and **be**:

$$X + \left\{ \begin{array}{l} \text{who} \\ \text{which} \\ \text{that} \end{array} \right\} + \text{tense} + \text{be} + Y \Rightarrow X + Y$$

Here are some more examples:

1. The book **(that is) lying on the floor** belongs to me.
2. The man **(who was) dragged through the streets** was no criminal.
3. The chair **(which is) behind the desk** is black.
4. The apartment **(that is) downstairs** is for rent.
5. John, **(who is) my brother,** is visiting me.
6. I saw a man **(who was) sound asleep.**
7. The man **(who is) to answer the question** has arrived.

As with other deletions, the rule allows us to recover the deleted material for each sentence. Transformations do not affect meaning, but they do alter the form of the sentence. Without deletion each of the above sentences contains a relative clause. If deletion occurs, the relative clause in sentence 1 becomes **lying on the floor**, a present participial phrase. Each of the reduced structures is named by its first word: **dragged through the streets** is a past participial phrase; **behind the desk** is a prepositional phrase; **downstairs** is an uninflected word used as an adverbial of place; **my brother** is a noun phrase used as an appositive; **sound asleep** is an adjective phrase; **to answer the question** is an infinitive phrase. We speak of all these structures collectively as *adjectivals*, since they all modify nouns.

Now look at the following deep structure: **Susan bought a car a car was red.** By the relative and Pro transformations this becomes **Susan bought a car which was red.** We may stop at this point, since any further transformations are optional. However, since the relative pronoun is followed by be, let us make the optional relative deletion transformation: **\*Susan bought a car red.** Unlike the sentences in the earlier paragraphs, this one is ungrammatical. Another transformation, however, will move the adjective red in front of car and give Susan bought a red car, which is grammatical and means the same thing as Susan bought a car which was red. This transformation, which we call the noun-modifier transformation (**NM**), moves an inflected single-word modifier to the position immediately in front of the noun:

$$X + N + NM + Y \Rightarrow X + NM + N + Y$$

This rule works for participles as well as for adjectives:

The boy who was yawning looked bored.

T-rel Del: The boy yawning looked bored.

T-NM:    The yawning boy looked bored.

As you can see from this example, rule T-NM is optional for most participles, although it is obligatory for adjectives. Many uninflected words do not undergo the noun-modifier transformation:

1. The people here are friendly.
2. *The here.people are friendly.

But some of them do:

1. The paragraph above is redundant.
2. The above paragraph is redundant.

Generally, adjectives with intensifiers may undergo this transformation:

1. He was a pitcher (who was) very good.

2. He was a very good pitcher.

Normally indefinite pronouns (someone, no one, everyone, everybody, etc.) block the noun-modifier transformation:

1. He found something (that was) unusual in the room.

2. *He found unusual something in the room.

In the rare sentence He found an unusual something in the room, something is functioning as a noun, not as an indefinite pronoun; notice the determiner **an**. Also, a few noun phrases that have been translated or borrowed from French do not permit this transformation: **the devil incarnate, court martial**, etc. For these cases the entire phrase will be entered in the lexicon as one unit.

Since a sentence may contain more than one NP, it may contain more than one relative clause or structure derived from a relative clause:

The **pretty** girl told a story **that was amusing** to the children **who were listening attentively.**

In this sentence three noun phrases have relative clauses embedded in them.

It is also possible to embed a relative clause inside another relative clause, as this tree shows:

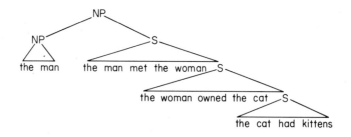

Transformed this will yield **the man who met the woman who owned the cat that had kittens.**

It would be theoretically possible for S to recur an infinite number of times. Our rules have made S a **recursive** element, like the rules that rewrite S and NP as $S^n$ and $NP^n$. A recursive element allows infinite reproduction of itself. Let us look at a sentence that has only limited repetition of S:

I met a man who had a son whose wife sold cookies that she had baked in her kitchen that was fully equipped with electrical appliances that were new.

As you can see from this sentence with only five relative clauses, a sentence that is extremely long is not pleasing from a stylistic point of view, and the reader or listener loses track of the meaning. But if we exclude such matters of performance as style and memory limitation and consider only the system, a sentence may be indefinitely long.

Now consider this sentence: **The little girl in the yard who steals peaches is a brat.** Our rule handles the NP easily:

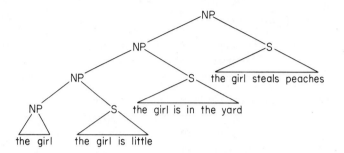

At times deletion can produce an ambiguous sentence in the surface structure: **I built the boat in the yard.** **In the yard** can tell where I built the boat, or it can tell which boat I built. The surface structure could be derived from either of the following:

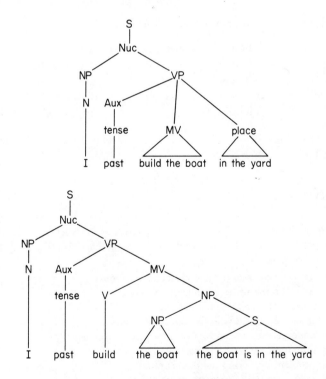

Surface structures are often structurally ambiguous; deep structures never are.

In this chapter we have considered several structures that result from the relative transformation:

1. The relative clause

| Deep structure: | The speech | you gave the speech | was good |
| T-rel: | The speech | the speech you gave | was good |
| T-pro: | The speech | that you gave | was good |

2. The relative clause with relative pronoun deleted

| Deep structure: | The speech | you gave the speech | was good |
| T-rel: | The speech | the speech you gave | was good |
| T-del: | The speech | you gave | was good |

3. The reduced relative clause: participial phrase, prepositional phrase, etc.

| Deep structure: | The man | the man was waiting for you | disappeared |
| T-rel: | The man | the man was waiting for you | disappeared |
| T-pro: | The man | who was waiting for you | disappeared |
| T-rel Del: | The man | waiting for you | disappeared |

4. The adjective and other pre-nominal modifiers

| Deep structure: | The car | the car is old | drives well |
| T-rel: | The car | the car is old | drives well |
| T-pro: | The car | that is old | drives well |
| T-rel Del: | The car | old | drives well |
| T-NM | The old car | | drives well |

These five transformations—Rel, Pro, Del, Rel Del, and NM—enable us to produce a large number of structures.

## exercises

A. In the following sentences classify each adjectival as to structure (relative clause, present participial phrase, etc.) and trace the sentence from its deep structure to the surface structure:

   1. The actor who made the speech looked nervous.
   2. He gave it to the usher seating the patrons.
   3. I read the book you recommended.
   4. He knows my cousin who lives in South Dakota.
   5. The announcement read in assembly was a surprise.
   6. He is the man we were talking about.
   7. The problem bothering me now is minor.
   8. The man at the door seemed worried.
   9. The stack counted by Jane was wrong.
  10. The yellow bird that was in the cage flew away.

B. In this chapter as in the rest of the book we have made much use of your knowledge of what is grammatical in leading you into generalizations about the language. Would this approach be effective if you were studying English as a foreign language? Explain.

C. Most single-word modifiers in English precede the noun, whereas phrases and clauses follow it. Is this true because of logic or convention?

D. Through the use of recursion, we can make a sentence infinitely long. Explain what limitations performance plays in sentence length. Do we have the same performance limitations in writing as in speech?

# chapter twelve
# SENTENCES
# AS NOUN PHRASES

In the last two chapters we have seen two different ways in which simple sentences may be expanded to make larger, more complex sentences: compounding and embedding. In compounding we add two or more Ss or NPs together, but they are distinct from each other; that is, in the deep structure we can always show on a tree where one S or NP ends and the other begins. Embedding, on the other hand, makes an S a part of another structure, such as an NP. In the deep structure underlying a relative clause, the S is one of the constituents of an NP. Through the use of embedding and compounding we can make sentences of any length or complexity that we choose.

Now examine the following sentences:

1. We know **who made the announcement.**
2. **What he said** was wrong.

In these sentences **who made the announcement** and **what he said** must be NPs, for we can substitute pronouns for them:

1a. We know **it.**
2a. **It** was wrong.

It is obvious that these NPs are sentences derived by the familiar WH transformation:

1b. NP-WH made the announcement      who made the announcement
2b. he said NP-WH                     what he said

Since our past rewrite rule for the NP will not permit these structures, let us revise it:

$$NP \rightarrow \begin{Bmatrix} (Det)\ N\ (Pl) \\ NP + S \\ NP^n \\ S \end{Bmatrix}$$

Instead of the other three choices, we may now select S:

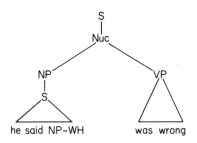

By the WH transformation this becomes

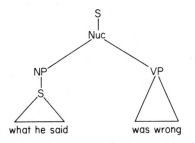

With the WH transformation we can derive other sentences:

1. We know      she did NP-WH
   We know      what she did
2. We know      she went Adv-m-WH
   We know      how she went
3. We know      she went Adv-r-WH
   We know      why she went
4. We know      she went Adv-t-WH
   We know      when she went
5. We know      she went Adv-p-WH
   We know      where she went
6. We know      she went with NP-WH
   We know      who she went with

This NP can function almost any way a single-word nominal can:

1. subject: **Whatever he said** was good.
2. direct object: We know **who opened the package.**
3. object of a preposition: They talked about **what she did.**
4. objective complement: She made him **what he is today.**
5. indirect object: He will give **whoever finished first** a prize.
6. subjective complement: The caller was **whom we had expected.**

The choice of WH words is the same for adverbials as it is for the WH transformation that produces questions. Only two possibilities exist for NPs, however: **who** for [ + human ] and **what** for [ − human ]. Any of the WH words except **why** may be followed by **ever**: **whoever, whatever,** etc.

Now look at the sentence **We know that she went. That** does not replace anything in the deep structure; **she went** is complete by itself. The word **that** has no meaning; rather, it is merely added to the nucleus as·a sentence modifier (cf. **The book that you bought is missing,** in which **that** means "the book" and is the direct object of **bought**). The deep structure for **We know that she went** is as follows:

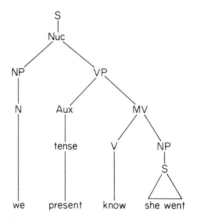

The WH transformation cannot apply, since no element in the deep structure has **WH** attached to it. We can apply the **that-insertion** transformation, however, to a sentence that is embedded as a noun phrase:

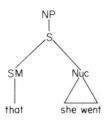

This gives **We know that she went.**

Any NP may be written as S, as the following tree shows with a subject NP:

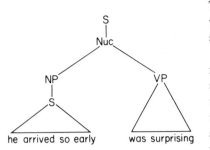

The **that**-insertion transformation will yield That he arrived so early was surprising.

There is another structure that means the same thing: For him to arrive so early was surprising. The transformation that produces for him to arrive so early does not merely add a subordinator to an otherwise unchanged nucleus, as does the one that attaches that. Previously we have gained insight into other structures by writing underlying structures above surface structures and deciding which transformational processes have been used: addition, deletion, rearrangement, substitution. Let us try this with the new structure:

| | | | | |
|---|---|---|---|---|
| Deep structure: | | he | past | arrive so early |
| Surface structure: | for | him | to | arrive so early |

The surface structure has two words added: for and to. Instead of arrived (past + arrive), it has arrive; hence, tense has been deleted. We call this transformation the **infinitive** transformation and for him to arrive so early an **infinitive phrase**.

There is another structure that is similar to that he arrived so early and for him to arrive so early: his arriving so early, as in the sentence His arriving so early was surprising. We call this structure a **gerund phrase**. Let us follow the same process as we did with the infinitive phrase to see how it is formed:

| | | | |
|---|---|---|---|
| Deep structure: | he | past | arrive so early |
| Surface structure: | he + poss | ing | arrive so early |

We say that his is a case of the pronoun he plus the possessive morpheme; similarly, John's is John + poss, their is they + poss, etc. As in the infinitive transformation, tense has been deleted and something has been added; this time it is **poss** and **ing**.

We have seen three possible transformations for he arrived so early and other sentences embedded as NPs:

1. that-insertion:   That he arrived so early was surprising.
2. infinitive:   For him to arrive so early was surprising.
3. gerund:   His arriving so early was surprising.

Other structures such as His early arrival was surprising could no doubt be derived by similar processes, but we will limit ourselves to these three.

In the sentence The idea that he would leave soon disturbed Sarah, that has obviously been added by the that-insertion transformation. Since that he would leave soon is not a relative clause, it cannot be derived from the S in the rule NP → NP + S. A final revision of the NP rule is required:

$$NP \rightarrow \left\{ \begin{array}{l} (Det)\ N\ (Pl)\ (S) \\ NP + S \\ NP^n \\ S \end{array} \right\}$$

The idea that he would leave soon is derived from NP → (Det) N (Pl) (S) as follows:

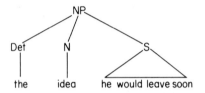

Compare this with the relative clause in The idea that he mentioned disturbed Sarah:

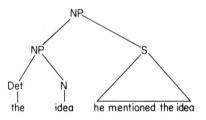

This new source will account for the following structures:

1a. The thought that I would be on time pleased me.
2a. The realization that he couldn't remember her name embarrassed Joe.

Instead of these surface structures, we could have the following:

1b. The thought pleased me that I would be on time.
2b. The realization embarrassed Joe that he couldn't remember her name.

Since these two sentences mean the same thing as their counterparts above and since they contain the same lexical items, they must have common deep structures. We say that sentences 1b and 2b have undergone an additional transformation, the **extraposition** transformation. This transformation moves an embedded sentence such as that I would be on time to the end of the sentence. We may illustrate extraposition by means of a tree. After that insertion we have the following intermediate structure:

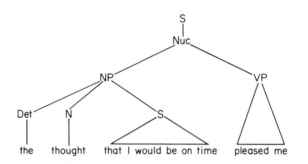

The extraposition transformation moves the embedded sentence to the end:

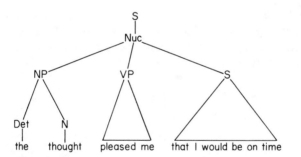

Now look at the following pairs of sentences:

3a. That he is leaving is unfortunate.
 b. It is unfortunate that he is leaving.
4a. That you are alone seems sad.
 b. It seems sad that you are alone.

These sentences seem to share the same relationships as those in the preceding paragraph did. Sentences 3a and 3b share the same deep structure; the extraposition transformation has been applied to 3b, but not to 3a. The same relationship is true for 4a and 4b.

After that insertion applies, we have the following intermediate structure:

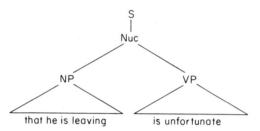

Extraposition rearranges the structure as follows:

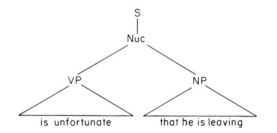

But *Is unfortunate that he is leaving is not a grammatical sentence. English insists upon something functioning as an NP at the beginning of most sentences, except in such obvious cases as imperatives. We, therefore, apply the it-insertion transformation:

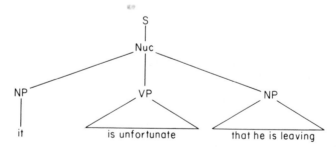

It has no lexical meaning and cannot, therefore, be in the deep structure. It is merely a filler, like do.

Often infinitive phrases may also undergo the extraposition transformation:

| Deep structure: | he arrived so early | was surprising |
| T-inf: | for him to arrive so early | was surprising |
| T-extrap: | was surprising | for him to arrive so early |
| T-it: | it was surprising | for him to arrive so early |

Sometimes relative clauses may undergo extraposition. Hence, **The idea that he suggested was exciting** may become **The idea was exciting that he suggested.**

In discussing compound sentences and relative clauses, we said that repeated words are normally deleted or replaced by Pro forms. Deletion applies also to infinitive and gerund phrases:

| | | |
|---|---|---|
| Deep structure: | John's ambition is | John becomes president |
| T-inf: | John's ambition is | for John to become president |
| T-del: | John's ambition is | to become president |

| | | |
|---|---|---|
| Deep structure: | Jane's worst fault is | Jane arrives late |
| T-gerund: | Jane's worst fault is | Jane's arriving late |
| T-del: | Jane's worst fault is | arriving late |

In addition to repeated words, indefinite pronouns may also be deleted: **For anyone to like him is impossible** becomes **To like him is impossible.**

Since structures resulting from the **that,** infinitive, and gerund transformations are dominated by the NP node, we expect them to behave as other NPs do. The structures we have considered so far do so, as the passive transformation shows:

1a. The judges ignored **what he said.**
 b. **What he said** was ignored by the judges.

2a. Everyone recognized **that he was telling the truth.**
 b. **That he was telling the truth** was recognized by everyone.

Now look at these sentences:

3a. Fred tends **to trust everyone.**
 b. *To trust everyone is tended by Fred.
4a. He needs **to stop the car.**
 b. *To stop the car is needed by him.

**To trust everyone** and **to stop the car** must be derived from **Fred trusts everyone** and **he stops the car** by the infinitive and deletion transformations, but they cannot be NPs or the sentences could undergo the passive transformation. **Fred tends to trust everyone** must come from a deep structure like this:

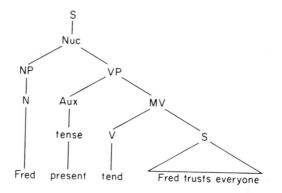

S is not classified as an NP. The rewrite rule for the MV must be expanded
for this type of structure:

$$MV \rightarrow \left\{ \begin{array}{l} be \left\{ \begin{array}{l} NP \\ AP \\ place \end{array} \right\} \\ \dot{V} \ (NP) \ (S) \end{array} \right\}$$

We may select V rather than **be** and only S after V, since NP is in parentheses.

This expansion of the MV rule will also account for an embedded S
following an NP:

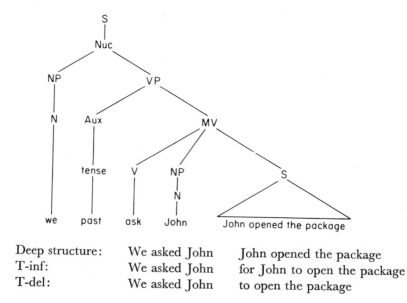

Deep structure:      We asked John      John opened the package
T-inf:               We asked John      for John to open the package
T-del:               We asked John      to open the package

This origin of **to open the package** correctly shows that it is not part of the NP containing **John**. Hence, the passive transformation moves only **John** to the beginning of the sentence: **John was asked by us to open the package.** If **to open the package** were part of the NP that contains **John**, the passive transformation would move the entire NP: *__John to open the package was asked by us.__ This kind of embedding is directly linked to verb features, since only certain verbs permit it: **ask, persuade, caution,** etc.

Now examine the following structure:

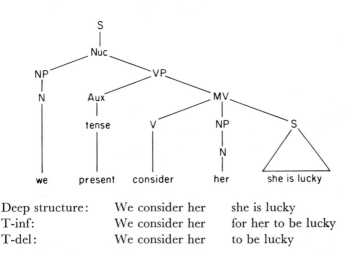

| Deep structure: | We consider her | she is lucky |
| --- | --- | --- |
| T-inf: | We consider her | for her to be lucky |
| T-del: | We consider her | to be lucky |

There is another kind of deletion which we encountered with the relative transformation. This is the transformation that deletes relative pronoun, tense, and **be** in a structure such as **who was waiting for you** to produce **waiting for you.** This transformation can be extended to sentences that have undergone the infinitive transformation, so that the following derivation is possible:

| Deep structure: | We consider her | she is lucky |
| --- | --- | --- |
| T-inf: | We consider her | for her to be lucky |
| T-del: | We consider her | lucky |

Since **We consider her to be lucky** and **We consider her lucky** mean the same thing, this transformation seems to be correct.

The same procedures will produce such structures as **She seems to be happy** and **She seems happy.**

| Deep structure: | She seems | she is happy |
| --- | --- | --- |
| T-inf: | She seems | for her to be happy |
| T-del: | She seems | to be happy |

Or by the other deletion transformation:

| Deep structure: | She seems | she is happy |
| T-inf: | She seems | for her to be happy |
| T-del: | She seems | happy |

With this chapter we are ending our consideration of syntax. We have seen that a small number of phrase-structure rules provide the deep structures for the sentences of English. Some of these rules include recursive elements:

1. Compounding:  $S \rightarrow S^n$

   $NP \rightarrow NP^n$

2. Verb Phrase Embedding:  $MV \rightarrow V$ (NP) (S)

3. Noun Phrase Embedding:  $NP \rightarrow$ (Det) N (Pl) (S)

   $NP \rightarrow S$

   $NP \rightarrow NP + S$

Lexical items from the dictionary are attached to the deep structure, and the semantic component assigns a meaning to it. This deep structure next undergoes one or more transformations, which perform any of four processes: addition, deletion, substitution, or rearrangement. The result is a surface structure. All that is needed now is a section of the grammar that tells us how to pronounce the surface structure. This is the phonological component, which will be the subject of Part Four of this book.

### exercises

A. Give the deep structure from which each of the following sentences was derived and show which transformations have been applied:
1. We didn't understand why you disagreed with us.
2. We admired his telling the truth.
3. Bill found a rare coin and sold it.
4. The suggestion that you made was interesting, but the proposal that we should leave wasn't.
5. It is good that you memorized their address.
6. Ann wanted to drive the car.
7. It is hard for me to remember names.
8. We persuaded Frank to answer the letter.
9. They considered your report to be very original.
10. Sue appears uneasy.

B. The transformations we have presented are representative rather than exhaustive of all of those necessary for English. With the knowledge you now have, you should be able to provide rules to account for the structures in sans serif in the following sentences:

1. We left **after the game was over.**
2. They left **because they were bored.**
3. I found the car **where you had parked it.**
4. **After the game was over,** we left.
5. **Because they were bored,** they left.

C. As a review of syntax, trace the steps by which the following sentence was derived: **Why didn't you tell those boys to be quiet?** Draw a tree to show the deep structure, show how lexical items are added, and perform the relevant transformations. How did you know which transformations to perform?

part four

*PHONOLOGY*

# chapter thirteen
## *TRANSCRIPTION*

We have studied in some detail the syntactic component of English transformational grammar. Although there still needs to be much further
research performed on English syntax, it will probably result in additions
to the grammar, rather than major revisions of the material that we have
presented. The syntactic component first generates a deep structure to
which the semantic component assigns meaning; this deep structure then
is converted into a surface structure by means of transformations. This
gives us a meaningful structure with its syntactic structure mapped out for
us; but it still is not in its final form, since we do not know how to pronounce
the sentence and since we still have such structures as *past + drop, bird +
Pl*, etc. We now turn to the phonological component, which gives the
sentence its final form and which turns an abstraction into a physical
actualization.

Anyone trying to discuss the sounds of English has problems if he tries
to use the conventional English alphabet. One letter may represent different
sounds in various words: the letter c does not indicate the same sound in
core as it does in cent; ch does not sound the same in champion, champagne,
or choir; i does not indicate the same sound in mine as it does in machine.
Also, one sound may be represented by different letters in various words;
we can see this by examining the vowel sound in the following words: meat,
mete, meet, field, receive, Caesar, amoeba, people, key, quay, pity,
machine. Since there are only 26 letters in our alphabet but 35 distinct
sounds generally heard in English, the conventional alphabet is inadequate
for precise description.

Some people have tried to alleviate this difficulty by using such
descriptions as "broad a" or "flat a." Unfortunately, there has never been
universal agreement as to which sounds are meant by these descriptions.
Other attempts have been made to identify a particular sound by the use of
key words. Problems arise when a sound is described as the "vowel heard
in root" or as the "final sound heard in father," since there is much variation

in the pronunciation of these words. Even when words with relatively little variation in pronunciation are used, it is vexatious to have to say something like "the vowel heard in bit" if many sounds are to be described. A much simpler system has been devised: a new alphabet. In this alphabet there is a unique symbol for each of the 35 sounds heard in English. Conventional spelling is ignored. The symbol /k/, for example, is used for the initial consonant heard in both cat and keep, as well as the same sound heard in account, back, chiropractor, acquaint, sacque, biscuit, and liquor (spelled cc, ck, ch, cq, cque, cu, and qu respectively). Furthermore, anyone trained in the use of this alphabet understands immediately the meaning of each symbol, whether he speaks the variety of English common in Boston, Houston, Kansas City, San Francisco, Melbourne, or London. We say that there is a perfect "fit" between this alphabet and the sounds it represents: each symbol invariably represents only one sound, and each sound has only one symbol that represents it. The alphabet used in this book is similar to the various American modifications that have been made of the International Phonetic Alphabet. We avoid using the pronunciation systems used by most dictionaries, since these systems vary from one dictionary to another. The account of phonology given in this chapter is overly simplified and in many ways outdated; however, the background provided is useful for an understanding of the transformational account that begins with Chapter Fourteen.

In this alphabet, which we call the **phonemic alphabet**, symbols for individual **phonemes** are placed between slanted lines, as /p/, to distinguish them from letters of the conventional alphabet, which are italicized or written in sans serif type. The symbol /p/ is used to indicate the consonant sound heard in pea and pay. Similarly, each of the following symbols is used to represent the first consonant heard in the words following it:

| | |
|---|---|
| /t/ | to, top, tie, town, tot |
| /k/ | kit, keep, cot, cab, come |
| /b/ | boy, bib, big, bat, by |
| /d/ | down, do, did, dog, Dan |
| /g/ | get, goose, give, gun, guess |

Notice that the sound heard at the beginning of gem and general although spelled with a g has a different sound from the first of got or give; the sound heard in gem and general will, therefore, not be represented by /g/, but by another symbol that will be introduced later.

The symbols for the vowel sounds may present a slight problem, since the English spelling system uses considerable variation in representing each vowel. At the beginning of this chapter, we gave twelve different spellings for the vowel sound heard in me and key. Regardless of how this sound is spelled, in the phonemic alphabet it is always presented as /i/. With this system me is written /mi/, key /ki/.

The vowel sound heard in did, hit, and kick has less variation in the ways it is normally spelled; the symbol for it is /ɪ/. The three words given as examples in the preceding sentence are written as follows: /dɪd/, /hɪt/, and /kɪk/.

## exercises

A. With these symbols for six consonants and two vowels, you are now able to transcribe the following words into phonemic notation:

| | | | |
|---|---|---|---|
| 1. pit | 12. keep | 23. bead | 34. peep |
| 2. Pete | 13. kit | 24. big | 35. pip |
| 3. pick | 14. keyed | 25. dip | 36 it |
| 4. peak | 15. kid | 26. deep | 37. eat |
| 5. peek | 16. bip | 27. Dick | 38. eke |
| 6. pig | 17. beep | 28. dig | 39. pea |
| 7. tip | 18. bit | 29. gig | 40. tea |
| 8. tick | 19. beet | 30. did | 41. tee |
| 9. teak | 20. beat | 31. deed | 42. key |
| 10. Teague | 21. beak | 32. bib | 43. be |
| 11. Kip | 22. bid | 33. kick | 44. bee |

B. Write the following in conventional English spelling:

| | | | |
|---|---|---|---|
| 1. /tik/ | 6. /pik/ | 11. /kid/ | 16. /pɪp/ |
| 2. /dɪp/ | 7. /pit/ | 12. /kɪd/ | 17. /did/ |
| 3. /bi/ | 8. /pɪg/ | 13. /bit/ | 18. /dɪd/ |
| 4. /it/ | 9. /tɪp/ | 14. /dip/ | 19. /bɪg/ |
| 5. /bɪp/ | 10. /kip/ | 15. /bɪb/ | 20. /bid/ |

C. Write each italicized vowel sound in phonemic transcription; do not be concerned with the rest of each word:

| | | | |
|---|---|---|---|
| 1. m*e* | 4. cl*ea*n | 7. w*o*men | 10. p*eo*ple |
| 2. bel*ie*ve | 5. g*ui*ld | 8. Ph*oe*nix | |
| 3. b*u*sy | 6. part*y* | 9. C*ae*sar | |

Most of the consonant symbols are easy to learn, since there is little variation in the spelling of consonants in English and since the phonemic symbols for 17 of the 24 consonant sounds are identical with the printed letters that normally spell these sounds. The following phonemic symbols represent the initial sounds heard in the words given after them:

/f/     fat, fig, fudge, phone, photo
/v/     vat, vain, vast, void, vice
/s/     sip, soup, sap, soap, seat
/z/     zoo, zany, zip, zebra, xylophone
/š/     shall, sheep, shoe, sugar, sure

Only the last symbol will be new. A few seconds of experimentation should convince you that this is indeed one sound, although we normally spell it with two letters: sh. Notice the position of your tongue when you pronounce /s/ as in sip and then /š/ as in ship. Then try pronouncing /s/ and immediately after it /h/, the sound heard at the beginning of how. The tongue position for /š/ is different from that for /s/ or /h/.

We are now ready to present three new vowel sounds with key words to show how they are pronounced:

/e/     late, may, steak, bait, rave
/ɛ/     pet, set, sell, neck, wet
/æ/     cat, bad, rag, lack, fast

In transcribing a word into phonemic script, be careful not to let the spelling confuse you. Pay special attention to the vowels. Notice that you are recording only the sound that you hear, not the conventional spelling. Notice the words be and bee, for example. Although the second of these words is spelled with two e's, there is no difference in pronunciation between it and the first word, be; both are, therefore, transcribed /bi/. If we had included the girl's name Bea for transcription, it would have been recorded the same: /bi/. Notice that capitalization is merely an orthographic device and is not indicated in our transcription since it is not heard. If a person says /bi/, it could be any of the three: be, bee, or Bea, as well as the name given in English to the letter of the alphabet, b. Similarly, we do not transcribe letters that are silent, as the g in gnat or the final e in Pete. Since Pete and peat are pronounced alike, they should both be transcribed /pit/. Finally, notice that only one /s/ sound occurs at the end of a word like pass, which is transcribed /pæs/.

## exercises

A. Transcribe the following words into phonemic notation:

| | | | |
|---|---|---|---|
| 1. fit | 14. sit | 27. Shick | 40. fizz |
| 2. feet | 15. seat | 28. sheik | 41. sheaf |
| 3. feat | 16. sick | 29. shake | 42. chef |
| 4. fate | 17. seek | 30. shack | 43. steak |
| 5. fact | 18. sack | 31. fish | 44. said |
| 6. fake | 19. sake | 32. bag | 45. sad |
| 7. fib | 20. Sid | 33. face | 46. shave |
| 8. egg | 21. gave | 34. says | 47. zigzag |
| 9. vet | 22. ship | 35. seize | 48. vast |
| 10. bad | 23. sheep | 36. cess | 49. vest |
| 11. vague | 24. Shep | 37. cease | 50. best |
| 12. sip | 25. shape | 38. see | |
| 13. seep | 26. sheet | 39. sea | |

B. Write the following words in conventional spelling:

| | | | |
|---|---|---|---|
| 1. /fek/ | 6. /šep/ | 11. /kæt/ | 16. /pev/ |
| 2. /fɪb/ | 7. /fɪš/ | 12. /siz/ | 17. /kev/ |
| 3. /ti/ | 8. /fez/ | 13. /sis/ | 18. /pes/ |
| 4. /sɪp/ | 9. /fes/ | 14. /šiv/ | 19. /kæst/ |
| 5. /šɪp/ | 10. /gæsp/ | 15. /iz/ | 20. /pe/ |

C. Write the italicized vowel sounds in phonemic notation:

| | | | |
|---|---|---|---|
| 1. l*ea*ther | 4. h*ei*fer | 7. b*u*ry | 10. s*ai*d |
| 2. v*ei*l | 5. l*eo*pard | 8. g*au*ge | |
| 3. st*ea*k | 6. p*ai*n | 9. m*ay* | |

The next group of new phonemic symbols is similar to the last group in that only one unusual consonant symbol is introduced:

| | |
|---|---|
| /r/ | red, ring, rust |
| /l/ | let, list, lamb |
| /m/ | man, money, moon |
| /n/ | now, noon, nurse |
| /ŋ/ | sing, rang, hung (the last sound in these words) |

The sound /ŋ/, although frequently spelled with the two letters **ng**, is in reality only one sound, not a combination of /n/ and /g/. Try pronouncing **run** and then **rung** and notice the tongue position at the end of each of these words. After you have established this difference, pronounce **run** and add a /g/ after the /n/. Now notice the pronunciation of **finger** and **singer**.

**Finger** has two consonant sounds in the middle: /ŋg/; **singer** has only one: /ŋ/. Try pronouncing **finger** with only the /ŋ/ and **singer** with /g/ after the /ŋ/.

Another potential source of difficulty is found in such words as **sink** and **pink**. Pronounce each of these words slowly and notice the movements of the tongue. As you pronounce **sin** and then **sing**, you will notice /n/ at the end of **sin** and /ŋ/ at the end of **sing**. For some speakers the vowel heard in **sing** is that of **seen**, not **sin**. Now try adding the sound /k/ at the end of **sin** and **sing**. The sound /k/ added to **sin** gives /sɪnk/, which is not a recognizable English word; but if this sound is added to the end of **sing**, the result is **sink**, which we write phonemically /sɪŋk/. A comparison of **pin** /pɪn/, **ping** /pɪŋ/, and **pink** /pɪŋk/ reveals the same sound contrasts.

Below are three new vowel sounds with key words to show how they are pronounced:

/ʌ/   cut, shirt, putt, mother
/ʊ/   full, put, could, hook
/u/   fool, Sue, true, moon

In **mother** there are two vowels. Although they sound alike to you, for reasons that will be made clear in a later chapter, we will transcribe this sound /ʌ/ when it is in a stressed syllable and /ə/ when it is unstressed: /mʌðər/.

## exercises

A.  Transcribe the following words:

| | | | |
|---|---|---|---|
| 1. mean | 14. sink | 27. but | 40. dirt |
| 2. man | 15. pink | 28. boot | 41. bank |
| 3. tin | 16. ping | 29. cake | 42. flood |
| 4. tan | 17. null | 30. blood | 43. two |
| 5. ton | 18. lose | 31. book | 44. move |
| 6. run | 19. loose | 32. tongue | 45. zest |
| 7. rung | 20. rude | 33. put | 46. sure |
| 8. rug | 21. fruit | 34. putt | 47. plaid |
| 9. loom | 22. took | 35. pert | 48. pled |
| 10. lung | 23. bury | 36. group | 49. laugh |
| 11. seen | 24. should | 37. shove | 50. does |
| 12. sin | 25. fool | 38. pain | |
| 13. sing | 26. full | 39. pang | |

B.  When a word contains more than one syllable, one of the syllables is pronounced louder and more forcefully than the others. We call this phenomenon *stress* (some books use the term *accent*). Although there are various ways of marking stress, in this book we shall use an acute mark over the vowel of the syllable containing the strongest stress: /kǽbɪn/. Transcribe the following words into phonemic symbols and mark the syllable with the strongest stress; remember to distinguish between stressed /ʌ/ and unstressed /ə/:

| | | | |
|---|---|---|---|
| 1. above | 7. (to) permit | 13. canoe | 19. stinger |
| 2. capital | 8. (a) permit | 14. pressure | 20. malinger |
| 3. capitol | 9. (to) survey | 15. padding | 21. anger |
| 4. singing | 10. pruning | 16. pudding | 22. tinkle |
| 5. (to) suspect | 11. easily | 17. precious | 23. tingle |
| 6. (a) suspect | 12. shouldn't | 18. finger | 24. parliament |

C. Which vowel is found more often than any other in unstressed position? Which of the following consonant sounds is never found at the beginning of a word in English: /m n ŋ r l/? Do all of them occur at the end?

D. Among speakers of English there is considerable variation in the pronunciation of such words as **root, coop,** and **hoof.** On separate paper draw three columns: (1) for words with /u/ as in **food,** (2) for words with /ʊ/ as in **took,** (3) for words with /ʌ/ as in **cut.** Determine which vowel you use in each of the following words and write the word in the appropriate column: **hoof, tool, cook, root, look, coop, kook, love, hood, mood, mud, Cooper, trooper, stood, move, hoop, proof, roof, shove, soot.**

E. Write the following in conventional English spelling:

| | | | |
|---|---|---|---|
| 1. /rɪŋ/ | 6. /kɪd/ | 11. /sprɪŋ/ | 16. /sɪŋ/ |
| 2. /mæd/ | 7. /kɪd/ | 12. /blum/ | 17. /lɪŋk/ |
| 3. /kʊd/ | 8. /šæl/ | 13. /plʌm/ | 18. /kɪŋk/ |
| 4. /kud/ | 9. /mæš/ | 14. /pruf/ | 19. /skræm/ |
| 5. /kʌd/ | 10. /ruf/ | 15. /strʌŋ/ | 20. /stɪŋk/ |

You should have no more trouble recognizing the remaining sounds than you had with the preceding ones; but since several of them are represented by symbols that will be new to you, we shall take them a little more slowly than we did those in the other exercises.

The initial sound heard in **hit, her,** and **house** is represented as /h/ and the initial sound in **wet, wear,** and **west** as /w/. These sounds by themselves will give you no trouble, but when the two come together you should be careful. The transcription of **hot** /hat/ and **watt** /wat/ are as you would probably expect. Now pay close attention to **what.** Ignoring the spelling and noticing only the shape of your mouth as you pronounce the word slowly several times, you will see that /h/ precedes /w/; hence, **what** is written /hwat/. For some speakers of English, the /h/ has been lost so that **what** and **watt** sound alike, as do **witch** and **which, where** and **wear.** Notice these sounds carefully as you transcribe the following words, using your usual pronunciation:

| | | | |
|---|---|---|---|
| 1. wet | 4. where | 7. heel | 10. whiff |
| 2. hail | 5. wear | 8. wheel | |
| 3. whale | 6. hash | 9. who | |

The initial sound heard in **yet, you,** and **young** is represented as /y/. Notice this sound at the beginning of **you,** and then pronounce the verb **use** carefully. The only difference in pronunciation of these two words is that **use** has a /z/ at the end of it. We write **you** as /yu/ and **use** as /yuz/. Do not let spelling confuse you; notice that there is no difference in pronunciation of **use** and the plural of **you** that is sometimes heard in the northeastern part of the United States: **youse.** We also call the letter of the alphabet **u** /yu/, not just /u/. The pronunciation /uz/ gives the word **ooze.** The three sounds /y, w, h/ are called *glides.* Transcribe the following words, giving your normal pronunciation:

| | | | |
|---|---|---|---|
| 1. few | 4. yes | 7. suit | 10. use (N) |
| 2. beauty | 5. moo | 8. do | |
| 3. booty | 6. music | 9. unit | |

The next sound is the consonant heard in the middle of **pleasure, measure,** and **seizure.** This sound is represented as /ž/. For many speakers of English it is the final sound heard in **beige, loge, rouge,** and **garage.** Transcribe the following words:

| | | | |
|---|---|---|---|
| 1. vision | 4. racer | 7. dilution | 10. composure |
| 2. fishing | 5. razor | 8. delusion | |
| 3. measure | 6. mirage | 9. composer | |

If you pronounce /t/ and /š/ together rapidly, you will have the initial sound in **child** and **chew.** For English this combination functions as one phoneme, which we write /č/. **Chew** is written /ču/ and **chum** /čʌm/. In a word like **clutch** be careful not to record a separate /t/, since this sound is included in the /č/. This word is written /klʌč/. A similar combination is that of /d/ and /ž/, the sound heard both at the beginning and at the end of *judge,* which we write /ǰ/. *Judge,* then, is written /ǰʌǰ/. Be careful not to write /d/ after the vowel, since this sound is included in the /ǰ/. The two sounds /č/ and /ǰ/ are called *affricates.* Transcribe the following words:

| | | | |
|---|---|---|---|
| 1. church | 6. fudge | 11. pleasure | 16. virgin |
| 2. chap | 7. hedge | 12. pledger | 17. version |
| 3. chafe | 8. fetch | 13. cheek | 18. badge |
| 4. gyp | 9. Dutch | 14. witch | 19. chunk |
| 5. Jeff | 10. peach | 15. which | 20. age |

The next two consonants are both spelled th. That they are distinct sounds can be clearly seen by comparing thy and thigh, either and ether, mouth (V) and mouth (N). The sound heard in thy, either, and mouth (V) is represented /ð/; the sound heard in thigh, ether, and mouth (N) is represented /θ/. When you pronounce /ð/, listen for the "buzzing" sound and hold your fingers on your throat to feel the vibration. This sound and vibration are absent in /θ/. Transcribe the following words:

| | | | |
|---|---|---|---|
| 1. teeth (N) | 6. the | 11. other | 16. north |
| 2. teethe (V) | 7. bath | 12. thanks | 17. northern |
| 3. faith | 8. bathe | 13. thug | 18. that |
| 4. thatch | 9. this | 14. thief | 19. thus |
| 5. these | 10. thistle | 15. with | 20. thesis |

The remaining vowel sounds can be easily handled in a list that includes key words:

/a/   father, hot, sock, top

/o/   hope, loaf, soak, grope

/ɔ/   ought, caught, fought

Some people pronounce *ought, caught,* and *fought* with the sound /a/ and have /ɔ/ in only a few words if they have it at all. One test to tell whether you use /ɔ/ is to see whether caught and cot, taught and tot sound alike or not. If they are different, then you have this sound; if they are alike, then you probably do not have it.

Finally, there are three diphthongs:

/au/   house, mouth, plow, about

/ai/   mice, right, kite, rise

/oi/   boy, oil, coy, point

There is much variation among speakers of English in the actual pronunciation of these sounds. Each person actually gives them varying pronunciations at different times. Whatever your exact pronunciation is, use the symbols we have given.

## exercises

A. Transcribe the following words:

| | | | |
|---|---|---|---|
| 1. pull | 14. think | 27. pot | 40. box |
| 2. pool | 15. ache | 28. pout | 41. Mark's |
| 3. pole | 16. daze | 29. pit | 42. Marx |
| 4. pile | 17. days | 30. pat | 43. sox |
| 5. pal | 18. queen | 31. put | 44. mule |
| 6. peel | 19. quit | 32. Pete | 45. jazz |
| 7. pale | 20. shout | 33. pet | 46. white |
| 8. pill | 21. coil | 34. shout | 47. wrong |
| 9. Paul | 22. thigh | 35. ouch | 48. purr |
| 10. extra | 23. thy | 36. joy | 49. loath |
| 11. exact | 24. choice | 37. rye | 50. loathe |
| 12. exaggerate | 25. choose | 38. work | |
| 13. excite | 26. mutt | 39. hurt | |

B. Write the names for the letters of the alphabet in phonemics: /e/, /bi/, /si/, etc.

C. Write the following in conventional English spelling:

| | | | |
|---|---|---|---|
| 1. /sop/ | 5. /sɪp/ | 9. /brɛd/ | 13. /brid/ |
| 2. /sæp/ | 6. /sup/ | 10. /brud/ | 14. /bred/ |
| 3. /sip/ | 7. /sofə/ | 11. /bræd/ | 15. /brɔd/ |
| 4. /sʌp/ | 8. /wɪmɪn/ | 12. /braid/ | 16. /braud/ |

D. Transcribe the following words:

| | | | |
|---|---|---|---|
| 1. breathe | 14. white | 27. foundling | 40. soiled |
| 2. nature | 15. surely | 28. collision | 41. fought |
| 3. plowed | 16. pleasure | 29. exaggerate | 42. sliced |
| 4. residential | 17. those | 30. voice | 43. creature |
| 5. book | 18. exact | 31. quota | 44. moth |
| 6. thigh | 19. loathes | 32. mighty | 45. explosion |
| 7. should | 20. applause | 33. said | 46. attacked |
| 8. musician | 21. wrong | 34. sugar | 47. pouch |
| 9. champagne | 22. appoints | 35. suggest | 48. pledger |
| 10. leisure | 23. badgers | 36. of | 49. pleasure |
| 11. plumber | 24. fox | 37. wharf | 50. joining |
| 12. view | 25. finger | 38. English | |
| 13. announced | 26. humiliation | 39. myth | |

# chapter fourteen
## PHONOLOGICAL FEATURES I†

Up to this point we have been concerned solely with learning a new alphabet for the transcription of sounds. For the rules which we will be making in the following chapters, we need more exact descriptions of the sounds. For our purposes the most effective descriptions are those of the functioning of various parts of the body in making sounds.

In English all speech sounds are made by modifying the flow of air as it is exhaled from the lungs. Although we make certain gasps and clicking sounds with air being inhaled, these are not part of our phonemic system. There are languages that do have phonemes formed by modifying air that is inhaled, but English does not. The first point at which we can modify the outflowing stream of air is in the larynx, which is popularly called the Adam's apple. In the larynx are two muscular bands which are wide apart during normal breathing. These bands, which we call the **vocal cords**, can be brought together to block the flow of air completely. We often do this when we are straining for some purpose, such as lifting a heavy load. Or we can bring them close together so that a vibration is set up when the air flows through them. This is done when we produce many of our speech sounds. These sounds are said to be **voiced**. If the vocal cords are wide enough apart so that no vibration occurs when air passes through them, the sound is **voiceless**. There are two different tests you can make to determine whether a sound is voiced or voiceless. You can hold your hand over your throat and pronounce a prolonged /z/. This should then be contrasted with a prolonged /s/. The other test is to pronounce each of these sounds while holding your hands lightly over your ears. Either test should reveal a definite vibration for /z/, but none for /s/; we, therefore, say that /z/ is voiced and /s/ voiceless. We described nouns and verbs by saying that they had or lacked certain features. We use a similar system with sounds; hence, /z/ has the feature [ + **voice** ] and /s/ has [ − voice ].

† This chapter is based on ideas found in Chapter Seven of *The Sound Pattern of English* by Noam Chomsky and Morris Halle (Harper & Row, Publishers, Incorporated, 1968).

Before going further, use either of the tests we have given to determine which of the following sounds have the feature [ + voice ] and which ones have [ — voice ]:

1. /z/     3. /v/     5. /i/     7. /ð/     9. /m/
2. /s/     4. /f/     6. /š/     8. /θ/     10. /h/

You should have found that the odd-numbered sounds are voiced and the even-numbered ones voiceless. Now try pronouncing each of these sounds again, but this time do not use your hand on your throat or over your ears. Listen for the difference in sound and see if you can feel the slight tension formed in the larynx for the voiced sounds.

The following sounds will be slightly harder, since they cannot be pronounced in isolation but always have a vowel (which is voiced) accompanying them. We normally call the letter of the alphabet **p** by the name /pi/. Since vowels are always voiced, you will hear the vibration when you say /pi/. If you notice carefully, however, you will find that voicing does not begin on the consonant /p/, but rather starts only with the vowel /i/. Contrast this word with /bi/; here voicing begins on the /b/. Classify the following sounds as [ + voice ] or [ — voice ]:

1. /p/     3. /t/     5. /k/     7. /č/
2. /b/     4. /d/     6. /g/     8. /ǰ/

All even-numbered sounds in this exercise have the feature [ + voice ], all odd-numbered ones [ — voice ].

For most sounds in English, the flow of air comes from the lungs and is released through the mouth after being altered by variations in the shape and positioning of the parts of the mouth. In the production of these sounds, the velum (the soft palate) is raised so that air will not go into the nasal passage, as it does in normal breathing. You can easily see the action of the velum if you look in a mirror as you breathe with your mouth open and then contrast this position with the one for the production of /a/. It is also possible to lower the velum and at the same time block the oral cavity with the lips or tongue, thereby forcing the air through the nasal passage. This is the way /m, n, ŋ/ are produced. You can tell that /m/ is a nasal consonant by pronouncing it protractedly and using your fingers to pinch the nose closed. As soon as you block the nose, the sound stops. Now try pronouncing /a/ or /s/ and pinch your nostrils together. The sound continues. For the production of /m/ the lips close the oral cavity; for /n/ the tip of the tongue blocks it by touching the gum ridge behind the upper teeth; for /ŋ/ the body of the tongue touches the velum. These three sounds have the feature [ + **nasal**]; all other sounds in English are [ — nasal ]. All nasal sounds in English also have the feature [ + voice ].

For all non-nasal sounds the flow of air passes through the mouth and is modified by the narrowing of two opposite parts (upper and lower lips, lower lip and upper teeth, tongue and velum, etc.). The degree of narrowing may be slight (cf. /e/ and /a/) or more extreme, sometimes to the point of complete closure. When you pronounce a consonant sound, you make an obstruction in the mouth. This obstruction may be complete closure, as in the production of /b, p, d, t, g, k/. We call these sounds *stops*, since the flow of air coming from the lungs is stopped at some point in the mouth and then released: between the two lips for /b/ and /p/, between the tongue tip and gum ridge for /d/ and /t/, between the body of the tongue and velum for /g/ and /k/. If there is a complete closure of the oral cavity, as in the production of the stops and the nasals, the sound is said to have the feature [ — **continuant** ]. Since /č/ and /ǰ/ are composed in part by /t/ and /d/, they also have this feature. All other sounds of English have the feature [ + continuant ], since the flow of air is not completely cut off in the oral cavity, but rather continues through it.

When you were in the first grade, you probably learned that the vowels are "a, e, i, o, and u and sometimes w and y." All other letters are consonants. This is a listing of **letters**, not **sounds**. English obviously has many more vowel sounds than this. Since this listing is rarely used for anything more than a memorization exercise that is an end in itself, it has normally not been challenged, even the use of w as a vowel. In the chapters that follow, we will need to make a more precise distinction between vowels and consonants, and we will concentrate on sounds rather than letters. We define a consonant sound as one with a radical obstruction in the oral cavity. The sounds we listed in the preceding paragraph as being [ — continuant ] all meet this condition. But this radical obstruction does not have to be so extreme as complete closure. The condition may also include a very narrow opening, such as that used in the production of /f, v, θ, ð, s, z, š, ž/. In the production of /r/, the tongue comes close enough to the palate to meet this condition. In the production of /l/, there is a radical obstruction with the tip of the tongue against the gum ridge, although the flow of air is not stopped as in the case of the noncontinuants but passes out over the sides of the tongue. All sounds with a radical obstruction have the feature [ + **consonantal**], usually abbreviated [ + cons ]. All others are [ — cons ]. Notice that the glides /y, w, h/ do not have an obstruction in their production and are, therefore, [ — cons ].

According to our system, a sound that is [ — cons ] is not necessarily a vowel. If you pronounce the following vowels in order, you will notice that your mouth is open relatively wide for /æ/ and that it becomes gradually narrower as you progress toward /i/: /æ, ɛ, e, ɪ, i/. You can see a similar progression with /a, ɔ, o, ʊ, u/. A sound is said to be [ + voc ] (i.e., **vocalic**) if it has a narrowing in the oral cavity no closer than that for /i/ and /u/. To give the rather general term *narrowing* more precision, we generally refer to this less extreme form of narrowing that does not exceed that for /i/ and /u/ as *constriction*. A narrowing that is extreme enough for the features that are [ + cons ] is called an *obstruction*. Therefore, all sounds that have a narrowing more severe than that of constriction are [ − voc ]. Notice that /y, w, h/ are [ − cons ] since there is no obstruction; similarly, they are [ − voc ] since they are pronounced with too severe a narrowing for constriction.

By using combinations of the features [ + cons ], [ − cons ], [ + voc ], and [ − voc ], we can divide the sounds in English into four kinds:

1. [ + cons ] and [ − voc ]: /p, b, t, d, k, g, č, ǰ, f, v, θ, ð, s, z, š, ž, m, n, ŋ/
2. [ − cons ] and [ + voc ]: /i, ɪ, e, ɛ, æ, a, ʌ, u, ʊ, o, ɔ/
3. [ − cons ] and [ − voc ]: /y, w, h/
4. [ + cons ] and [ + voc ]: /r, l/

The sounds /r/ and /l/ are obviously [ + cons ] because of the obstruction in the oral cavity. They are also classified as [ + voc ] because of certain operations of the vocal cords that are too technical for the scope of this book.

Sometimes we add another feature, [ + **sonorant** ] , which includes all sounds that are [ + voc ] as well as the glides /y, w, h/ and the nasals /m, n, ŋ/. All other sounds are [ − sonorant ]. Another name for [ − sonorant ] is **obstruent**.

We have said that a sound has the feature [ + cons ] if there is an obstruction in the oral cavity. If this obstruction is at the gum ridge or farther forward, the sound has the feature [ + **anterior** ]. The following [ + cons ] sounds have this feature: /p, b, t, d, s, z, f, v, θ, ð, m, n, l/. These are [ − anterior ]: /k, g, ŋ, š, ž, č, ǰ, r/. Since there is no obstruction in the production of the vowels and glides, they are [ − anterior ].

Another feature of consonants is determined by the position of the tongue. The part of the tongue that in a relaxed position lies opposite the alveolum (the gum ridge) is called the *blade*; the blade includes the tip of the tongue. If the blade of the tongue is raised above this relaxed position on the floor of the mouth, the sound has the feature [ + **coronal** ]. The sounds /t/ and /d/ are [ + coronal ], since the blade of the tongue touches the alveolum; /p/ and /b/, however, are [ − coronal ], since it is the lips that form the closure and the blade of the tongue is not affected. The velar sounds /k/ and /g/ are [ − coronal ], since it is the body of the tongue rather than the blade that is raised. Vowels are, of course, [ − coronal ], since their production does not involve the blade of the tongue.

Some consonant sounds are produced with an obstruction that is not complete closure but which is narrow enough to cause considerable noisiness as the air is forced out a narrow opening. These sounds are [ + **strident** ] and include the following: /f, v, s, z, š, ž, č, ǰ/.

We have classified sounds as [ + coronal ] or [ − coronal ] by the position of the blade of the tongue. We assign features also by the position of the *body* of the tongue, that part behind the blade. For normal breathing the body, like the blade, is relaxed and on the floor of the mouth. For the production of /e/, the blade of the tongue does not move, but the body is raised slightly. We use this position as a starting point in describing the feature of tongue position.

1. A sound produced with the body of the tongue raised above the position for /e/ is [ + **high** ]; all others are [ − high ]. If you notice the position of the body of your tongue as you pronounce the following sounds, you will see that they are [ + high ]: /i, ɪ, u, ʊ, y, w, k, g, ŋ, š, ž, č, ǰ/. All other sounds in English are [ − high ].
2. A sound produced with the body of the tongue lower than the position for /e/ is [ + **low** ]: /æ, a, ɔ, h/. All others are [ − low ] in English.
3. A sound produced with the body of the tongue farther back than the position of /e/ is [+ **back**] : /u, ʊ, o, ɔ, a, ʌ, w, k, g, ŋ/. All others are [ − back ].

All vowels have the features [ − cons ] and [ + voc ]; these features set them off from all other sounds. The three features high, low, and back help us to distinguish them from one another:

|      | i | ɪ | e | ɛ | æ | ɔ | a | u | ʊ | o | ʌ |
|------|---|---|---|---|---|---|---|---|---|---|---|
| high | + | + | − | − | − | − | − | + | + | − | − |
| low  | − | − | − | − | + | + | + | − | − | − | − |
| back | − | − | − | − | − | + | + | + | + | + | + |

These features differentiate some of the vowels, but not all. Notice the following groups:

1. $\begin{bmatrix} + \text{high} \\ - \text{low} \\ - \text{back} \end{bmatrix}$ /i, ɪ/

2. $\begin{bmatrix} - \text{high} \\ - \text{low} \\ - \text{back} \end{bmatrix}$ /e, ɛ/

3. $\begin{bmatrix} + \text{high} \\ - \text{low} \\ + \text{back} \end{bmatrix}$ /u, ʊ/

4. $\begin{bmatrix} - \text{high} \\ - \text{low} \\ + \text{back} \end{bmatrix}$ /o, ʌ/

5. $\begin{bmatrix} - \text{high} \\ + \text{low} \\ + \text{back} \end{bmatrix}$ /a, ɔ/

6. $\begin{bmatrix} - \text{high} \\ + \text{low} \\ - \text{back} \end{bmatrix}$ /æ/

Some vowels are produced with more tension and effort than others. The following are said to be [ + **tense** ]: /i, e, u, o, ɔ/. The others are [ − tense ], or lax. Some dialects have a lax /o/, and others have tense variants of /æ/ and /a/. The glides /y/ and /w/ are [ − tense ]. The tense vs. lax distinction is normally not extended to other sounds in English.

## exercises

A. List the features that the following pairs of sounds share:

| | | | |
|---|---|---|---|
| 1. /k, g/ | 6. /y, ǰ/ | 11. /i, u/ | 16. /y, i/ |
| 2. /f, v/ | 7. /s, z/ | 12. /u, ʊ/ | 17. /k, ʌ/ |
| 3. /m, b/ | 8. /p, t/ | 13. /a, ɔ/ | 18. /u, a/ |
| 4. /ð, z/ | 9. /d, č/ | 14. /e, o/ | 19. /æ, h/ |
| 5. /w, k/ | 10. /š, ž/ | 15. /o, a/ | 20. /u, w/ |

List the ways in which the following pairs of sounds differ:

| | | | |
|---|---|---|---|
| 1. /m, n/ | 6. /f, θ/ | 11. /v, s/ | 16. /a, ɔ/ |
| 2. /y, w/ | 7. /l, n/ | 12. /i, ɪ/ | 17. /æ, ɛ/ |
| 3. /r, l/ | 8. /k, ŋ/ | 13. /ɪ, ʊ/ | 18. /u, w/ |
| 4. /p, t/ | 9. /č, ǰ/ | 14. /r, æ/ | 19. /e, m/ |
| 5. /m, b/ | 10. /d, g/ | 15. /ð, ɛ/ | 20. /š, ž/ |

C. Our grammar contains three components: syntax, semantics, and phonology. In which of these will performance differ the most from competence? Name several distorting factors on performance.

# chapter fifteen
# PHONOLOGICAL FEATURES II

As you saw in the last chapter, the production of speech involves the inter-
action of many parts of the vocal apparatus, the most prominent being the
vocal cords, the velum, and the tongue. The features give an account of
these actions. You are now able to understand that symbols such as /p, g, a/
are not indivisible units but rather *abbreviations* for feature complexes.
Instead of writing [ + cons, − voc, − continuant, + anterior, − coronal,
etc. ], we can write /p/ and let this symbol stand for this complex of features.

In the last chapter we discussed the thirteen features that are most
relevant for a study of English. These features are part of a listing of thirty
or forty that underlie all human languages. To give you some idea of the
other features, we will use two examples that can be readily observed.
When you pronounce /u, o, w/, you round your lips. Contrast these sounds
with /i, e, y/, for which there is no lip rounding. We could have given a
feature [ + **round** ], but we did not because in English all sounds that are
[ + round ] are also [ + back ]. The feature would not have been of any
real value in showing differences or similarities among sounds. But for some
languages, such as French, German, and Swedish, there are vowels that are
[ − back ] and [ + round ]; for these languages rounding is a significant
feature. As a second example, hold your hand in front of your mouth as you
pronounce /pæn/, /tæn/, and /kæn/. You should feel a puff of air, which we
call *aspiration*, accompanying /p, t, k/ in these words. This puff of air is
missing if /s/ precedes the consonant: /spæn/, /stæn/, and /skæn/. Since
aspiration is predictable at the beginning of a word after /p, t, k/ if /s/ does
not precede, the feature [ + aspirated ] is not significant for English. For
some other languages, such as Hindi, aspiration is significant, since it alone
can distinguish one sound from another.

The feature system can be applied to all languages. When we are
speaking of universal phonology as opposed to the phonological system of a
particular language, it is not adequate to list features merely plus or minus;
instead, they are given numbers on a scale: 1, 2, 3, etc. For example, we

will want to show that when aspiration is present, /p/ is more strongly aspirated than /k/ or that a sound that is [ + back ] may be farther back than another [ + back ] sound. In working with universal phonology, then, we will use all thirty or forty features and use numbers on a scale rather than plus or minus. In working with the phonology of a specific language, however, we will limit ourselves to the features that are significant for that language and use only plus and minus values.

Here are the features for the vowels of English as we presented them in the last chapter:

|            | i | ɪ | e | ɛ | æ | u | ʊ | o | ʌ | a | ɔ |
|------------|---|---|---|---|---|---|---|---|---|---|---|
| cons       | − | − | − | − | − | − | − | − | − | − | − |
| voc        | + | + | + | + | + | + | + | + | + | + | + |
| sonorant   | + | + | + | + | + | + | + | + | + | + | + |
| continuant | + | + | + | + | + | + | + | + | + | + | + |
| nasal      | − | − | − | − | − | − | − | − | − | − | − |
| anterior   | − | − | − | − | − | − | − | − | − | − | − |
| coronal    | − | − | − | − | − | − | − | − | − | − | − |
| high       | + | + | − | − | − | + | + | − | − | − | − |
| low        | − | − | − | − | + | − | − | − | − | + | + |
| back       | − | − | − | − | − | + | + | + | + | + | + |
| tense      | + | − | + | − | − | + | − | + | − | − | + |
| voice      | + | + | + | + | + | + | + | + | + | + | + |
| strident   | − | − | − | − | − | − | − | − | − | − | − |

Our matrix is redundant, since for English if we know that a segment is [ − cons ] and [ + voc ], we can predict certain other features: [ + sonorant, + continuant, − nasal, − anterior, − coronal, + voice, − strident ]. We can make our matrix much more economical in space if we are allowed to omit these features, but first we need a general rule that will reinsert them when they are needed:

$$
\begin{bmatrix} + \text{voc} \\ - \text{cons} \end{bmatrix} \rightarrow
\begin{bmatrix} + \text{voc} \\ - \text{cons} \\ + \text{sonorant} \\ + \text{continuant} \\ - \text{nasal} \\ - \text{anterior} \\ - \text{coronal} \\ + \text{voice} \\ - \text{strident} \end{bmatrix}
$$

This is the form that **redundancy** rules are stated in. The rule says that we rewrite all vowels with the features [ + sonorant, + continuant, etc. ].

The rule allows us to add these features to any vowel when we wish to include a full phonetic representation, including features redundant for English. Some of these features, such as [ + continuant, − anterior, − coronal, − strident ], are universal; others, such as [ − nasal ], apply only to English. Universal and language-specific rules should be kept distinct and in separate grammars. Because of space limitations, we have combined them.

Even with these redundancies removed, our matrix will still contain redundant information. All segments that are [ + high ] are necessarily [ − low ] because of the shape of the human tongue, and those that are [ + low ] are [ − high ]. Two rules will permit us to make further simplifications:

$$[ + \text{high} ] \rightarrow \begin{bmatrix} + \text{high} \\ - \text{low} \end{bmatrix}$$

$$[ + \text{low} ] \rightarrow \begin{bmatrix} + \text{low} \\ - \text{high} \end{bmatrix}$$

By leaving out the information provided for by the redundancy rules, we retain the following:

|       | i | ɪ | e | ɛ | æ | u | ʊ | o | ʌ | a | ɔ |
|-------|---|---|---|---|---|---|---|---|---|---|---|
| cons  | − | − | − | − | − | − | − | − | − | − | − |
| voc   | + | + | + | + | + | + | + | + | + | + | + |
| high  | + | + | − | − |   | + | + | − | − |   |   |
| low   |   |   |   | − | − | + |   |   | − | − | + | + |
| back  | − | − | − | − | − | + | + | + | + | + | + |
| tense | + | − | + | − | − | + | − | + | − | − | + |

In omitting redundant phonological features, we are following the same process that we used with lexical features. A complete lexicon would contain a redundancy rule such as the following for nouns:

$$[ + \text{human} ] \rightarrow \begin{bmatrix} + \text{animate} \\ + \text{concrete} \\ + \text{human} \end{bmatrix}$$

Future developments in transformational grammar will probably provide many more parallels between different components of the grammar.

Now let us review the other sounds and see what redundancies we can omit:

| | p | b | t | d | k | g | č | ǰ | f | v | θ | ð | s | z | š | ž | m | n | ŋ | r | l | h | y | w |
|---|---|---|---|---|---|---|---|---|---|---|---|---|---|---|---|---|---|---|---|---|---|---|---|---|
| cons | + | + | + | + | + | + | + | + | + | + | + | + | + | + | + | + | + | + | + | + | + | − | − | − |
| voc | − | − | − | − | − | − | − | − | − | − | − | − | − | − | − | − | − | − | − | + | + | − | − | − |
| continuant | − | − | − | − | − | − | − | − | + | + | + | + | + | + | + | + | − | − | − | + | + | + | + | + |
| nasal | − | − | − | − | − | − | − | − | − | − | − | − | − | − | − | − | + | + | + | − | − | − | − | − |
| anterior | + | + | + | + | − | − | − | − | + | + | + | + | + | + | − | − | + | + | − | + | + | − | − | − |
| coronal | − | − | + | + | − | − | + | + | − | − | + | + | + | + | + | + | − | + | − | − | + | − | − | − |
| high | − | − | − | − | + | + | + | + | − | − | − | − | − | − | + | + | − | − | + | − | − | − | + | + |
| low | − | − | − | − | − | − | − | − | − | − | − | − | − | − | − | − | − | − | − | − | − | + | − | − |
| back | − | − | − | − | + | + | − | − | − | − | − | − | − | − | − | − | − | − | + | − | − | − | − | + |
| voice | − | + | − | + | − | + | − | + | − | + | − | + | − | + | − | + | + | + | + | + | + | − | + | + |
| strident | − | − | − | − | − | − | + | + | + | + | − | − | + | + | + | + | − | − | − | − | − | − | − | − |
| sonorant | − | − | − | − | − | − | − | − | − | − | − | − | − | − | − | − | + | + | + | + | + | + | + | + |

The redundancies here are less obvious than those for the vocalic segments. Closer inspection will nevertheless reveal them. First of all, we gave rules stating that segments that are [ + high ] are automatically [ − low ] and those that are [ + low ] are [ − high ]. Now look at the segments that are [ + nasal ]. All of these segments are also [ − continuant, − low, + voice, − strident, + sonorant, + cons, − voc ] in English. A rule will permit us to omit this information:

$$[ + \text{nasal} ] \rightarrow \begin{bmatrix} + \text{cons} \\ - \text{voc} \\ + \text{nasal} \\ - \text{continuant} \\ - \text{low} \\ + \text{voice} \\ - \text{strident} \\ + \text{sonorant} \end{bmatrix}$$

Notice that this is a rule specifically for English, not a rule for all languages as is the one that states that [ + high ] is also [ − low ]. Next, notice that /r/ and /l/ are distinctively identified by the combination [ + cons ] and [ + voc ]; all that is needed for them is one further feature to distinguish them from each other: [ + anterior ] or [ − anterior ]. Similarly, segments that are [ − cons ] and [ − voc ] are [ − nasal, − anterior, − coronal, − strident, + sonorant ]. For English all segments that are [ + cons, − voc, − nasal ] are [ − low ] and [ − sonorant ]. These restrictions and several others will be stated in rules like the ones we have given. Omitting redundancies, we have the following matrix:

|  | p | b | t | d | k | g | č | ǰ | f | v | θ | ð | s | z | š | ž |
|---|---|---|---|---|---|---|---|---|---|---|---|---|---|---|---|---|
| continuant | − | − | − | − | − | − | − | − |  |  | + | + |  |  | + | + |
| nasal | − | − | − | − | − | − |  |  |  |  |  |  |  |  |  |  |
| anterior | + | + | + | + | − | − | − | − | + | + | + | + | + | + | − | − |
| coronal | − | − | + | + | − | − | + | + | − | − | + | + | + | + | + | + |
| voice | − | + | − | + | − | + | − | + | − | + | − | + | − | + | − | + |
| strident |  |  |  |  |  |  | + | + | + | + | − | − | + | + | + | + |

|  | m | n | ŋ | r | l | y | w | h |
|---|---|---|---|---|---|---|---|---|
| cons |  |  |  | + | + | − | − | − |
| voc |  |  |  | + | + | − | − | − |
| nasal | + | + | + |  |  |  |  |  |
| anterior | + | + | − | − | + |  |  |  |
| coronal | − | + |  |  |  |  |  |  |
| high |  |  |  |  |  | + | + | − |
| back |  |  |  |  |  | − | + |  |

Features that are not redundant are called **distinctive**. The distinctive features of a sound are those needed to identify it unambiguously from other sounds. Two sounds are different if they differ by at least one feature. For example, /p/ and /b/ share all except one feature: /p/ is [ − voice ] and /b/ is [ + voice ]; hence, only voice is distinctive in separating these sounds. Similarly, /t/ and /p/ differ only in that /t/ is [ + coronal ] and /p/ is [ − coronal ]. Voicing is distinctive for all nonnasal consonants in English; for nasals it is not.

The feature system reveals similarities among sounds more interesting than their differences. Features can be used to group sounds into classes. For example, only /r/ and /l/ have both [ + cons ] and [ + voc ]. These two features set them off from all other sounds in what we call a **natural class** of sounds. We need fewer features to specify a natural class than we do to specify any member of the class. To specify either /r/ or /l/ by itself, we need three features: [ + cons, + voc, − anterior ] and [ + cons, + voc, + anterior ], respectively.

Contrast this natural class with another pair of sounds: /d/ and /v/. These sounds have much in common: [ + cons, − voc, − nasal, + anterior, − high, + voice ]. But this is not sufficient to set them off from /b/, /ð/, and /z/, which share the same features. The only way we can talk about /d/ and /v/ together is to list all of the features for each; they are not a natural class. Notice that a mere listing of the symbols does not show the difference between the pairs /d, v/ and /r, l/; the feature system reveals the major differences.

We find motivation for natural classes outside of a discussion of features. As we will see in Chapter Eighteen, nouns ending in a sound with the features [ + strident, + coronal ] (e.g., church, dish, judge, etc.) take the plural /ɪz/. Verbs with the features [ − continuant, − nasal, + anterior, + coronal ] in their last segment take the past tense /ɪd/. There is also historical motivation for natural classes. During the fifteenth century, English segments with the features [ + voc, − cons, + tense ] underwent a major change in tongue height. Natural classes defined by distinctive features provide meaningful, linguistically significant generalizations about the sound system.

Phonological entries in a lexicon should be given as nonredundant matrices rather than as alphabetic abbreviations. Instead of listing mail as /mel/, we would list the following:

$$
\begin{bmatrix} + \text{nasal} \\ + \text{anterior} \\ - \text{coronal} \end{bmatrix}
\begin{bmatrix} - \text{cons} \\ + \text{voc} \\ - \text{high} \\ - \text{low} \\ - \text{back} \\ + \text{tense} \end{bmatrix}
\begin{bmatrix} + \text{cons} \\ + \text{voc} \\ + \text{anterior} \end{bmatrix}
$$

With nonredundant matrices we are not losing the other features: /l/ is still [ − nasal ], /m/ is still [ + voice ], etc. The matrix found in the lexicon will look like *1* below; redundancy rules will convert it into a fully specified form like *2* before any natural classes can be defined or any phonological rules, such as plural formation, can be applied:

|              | *1* | *2* |
|--------------|-----|-----|
| cons         |     | +   |
| voc          |     | −   |
| continuant   |     | −   |
| nasal        | +   | +   |
| anterior     | +   | +   |
| coronal      | −   | −   |
| high         |     | −   |
| low          |     | −   |
| back         |     | −   |
| voice        |     | +   |
| strident     |     | −   |
| sonorant     |     | +   |

The redundancy rules we have considered so far apply to any phoneme in English, regardless of which other phonemes surround it. English also has limitations on the sequences of phonemes that may occur. For example, there are no words in English that begin with consonant clusters such as /pt, fk, lz/, nor is this just an accidental omission that might soon be filled with new words. English permits only a few combinations of consonants at the beginning of a word. If a word begins with two segments that are both [ + cons ] and [ − voc ], only five possibilities exist: /sp, st, sk, sm, sn/. We can, therefore, state the following redundancy rule for /s/, using the symbol # outside the matrix to indicate initial position:

$$
\# \, [\, + \text{cons} \,]
\begin{bmatrix} + \text{cons} \\ - \text{voc} \end{bmatrix}
\rightarrow \#
\begin{bmatrix} + \text{cons} \\ + \text{anterior} \\ + \text{coronal} \\ - \text{voice} \\ + \text{strident} \end{bmatrix}
\begin{bmatrix} + \text{cons} \\ - \text{voc} \\ - \text{continuant} \end{bmatrix}
$$

In the position for /s/, all features except [ + cons ] have become **neutralized**; that is, they are not needed to distinguish /s/ from other sounds. Another rule in English says that of the nasals, only /m/ and /n/ may occur at the beginning of a word; this nasal must be followed by a vowel:

$$
\# \, [\, + \text{nasal} \,] \, [\quad] \rightarrow \#
\begin{bmatrix} + \text{nasal} \\ + \text{anterior} \end{bmatrix}
\begin{bmatrix} + \text{voc} \\ - \text{cons} \end{bmatrix}
$$

There are many constraints on the sequences of sounds that are permitted in English. A complete lexicon would contain a full listing of redundancy rules, both those that are context free and those that are contextually determined. The lexical entries would be free of all redundancies and would contain only the minimum number of features needed to identify morphemes unambiguously. The few words which do not observe these constraints, such as **sphere, svelte,** and **tsetse,** would be treated as exceptions; they would have a comment that certain redundancy rules are not to be applied. Rules will block all impossible words; they will not block any that are possible, even though they may not exist at present. Hence, rules will block /fnæt/ but not /spæd/, although neither is currently an English word.

A complete set of redundancy rules for English will do more than conserve space in the lexicon. It will state all the significant generalizations about the phonological patterns in the language and will define all possible morphemes, including potential ones that have not yet been formed.

We have observed that some phonological constraints are universal and others are peculiar to English. The study of universals in phonology has led some linguists to a different treatment of features. Some feature combinations, such as [ + high, + low ], and some sequences of segments, such as /wgb/, are inherently impossible to pronounce; others are impossible to perceive. Also, there are other feature combinations and segment sequences that are possible but very difficult to make or perceive. Some feature combinations and sequences are inherently more "natural" than others. All this can be embodied in universal rules applying to all languages. If any lexical item in a language obeys these rules, it is *unmarked*; if it disobeys these universal constraints, it is *marked* (i.e., it will take on the opposite specification from what the universal rule would predict). Since most feature specifications in most segments in most lexical items *are* predictable by general, universal rules, most feature specifications will be unmarked. This procedure will distinguish language-specific elements from universal elements in a particular language. Research on which feature combinations are natural and which unnatural is just in its beginning stages, but the future holds much promise.

## exercises

If the sounds grouped together constitute a natural class, give the features that distinguish them; if they do not constitute a natural class, do nothing with them:

1. /m, n, ŋ/
2. /p, b, m, f, v/
3. /s, z, š, ž, f, v, č, ǰ/
4. /y, w, h/
5. /p, b, t, d, r, s/
6. /k, g, ŋ, w/
7. /θ, s, č, y/
8. /t, d, č, ǰ, θ, ð/

9. /k, g, č, ǰ, š, ž, ŋ/
10. /r, l, h, y, w/
11. /i, ɪ, u, ʊ/
12. /u, ʊ, o, ʌ, a, ɔ/
13. /i, e, ʊ, ɔ/
14. /i, e, u, o, ɔ/
15. /i, ɪ, e, ɛ, æ/

# chapter sixteen
# *SYNTAX AND STRESS*†

In English as in many other languages, certain syllables are pronounced with more force than others. In a word one syllable will have the strongest force; in a phrase a syllable of one word will be the strongest. This extra force on a syllable is commonly called *accent*, a term which is often used for other meanings as well: pitch, strangeness of speech, etc. To avoid confusion with these other meanings, linguists usually use the word **stress** to name this added force that is given to a syllable or a word.

Lexical entries for most words will not include stress, since English stress patterns are normally predictable by rules such as those we will present in this chapter. Only words which do not follow these rules will have their stress patterns marked in the lexicon. This practice parallels that for noun plurals and past-tense forms of verbs, in which only exceptions such as **men** and **caught** are given in the lexicon.

Earlier, we spoke of certain vowels as having the feature [ + tense ] and others as [ − tense ]. This distinction of tense and lax is important for determining the placement of stress. Notice the position of the primary stress in the following words:

|              *1* |           *2* |
| --- | --- |
| surrénder | reláte |
| hínder | cajóle |
| pólish | repéat |
| whístle | escápe |
| astónish | maintáin |
| rélish | survíve |

Each of the verbs in the first column has a lax vowel in the ultimate (i.e., last) syllable; stress occurs not on this syllable, but on the penultimate

---

† This chapter is based on ideas found in Chapter Three of *The Sound Pattern of English* by Noam Chomsky and Morris Halle (Harper & Row, Publishers, Incorporated, 1968).

(next to last) syllable. The words in the second column all end in a syllable containing a tense vowel or diphthong; this tense vowel receives primary stress.

Now look at the adjectives in the two columns below:

|         *1*         |         *2*         |
|---------------------|---------------------|
| frágile             | sublíme             |
| régal               | secúre              |
| rígid               | políte              |
| explícit            | sevére              |
| púrple              | seréne              |

Adjectives obviously are governed by the same rules as verbs are: primary stress is placed on an ultimate tense vowel or diphthong; otherwise it goes on the penultimate syllable.

We can begin formulating a rule for placing stress in a word. In doing this we adopt certain notational conventions. A capital **C** will be our abbreviation for **consonant** or [ + cons, − voc ]; **Vw** will abbreviate **vowel**, [ − cons, + voc ] (we cannot use just **V** since that is our abbreviation for **verb**). The symbol $C_2^5$ will mean a cluster of at least two but not more than five consonants. The lower number means the minimum, the upper the maximum. If we do not want to state a maximum, we do not give an upper number; hence, $C_2$ means two or more consonants, no upper limit given. If we do not want to set a minimum, we use the notation $C_0$; this means no consonant, one consonant, or any number. Similarly, $C_0^2$ means no consonant, one consonant, or two consonants; $C_1^1$ means exactly one consonant, $C_2^2$ two consonants, etc. Instead of the last two symbols for an exact number of consonants, we normally omit the number and list C the number of times it is used: C (exactly one consonant), CC (two consonants), CCC (three consonants), etc. This convention saves a great deal of space. The symbol $VwC_0^3$ is an abbreviation for the following:

Vw
VwC
VwCC
VwCCC

We can now state our rule for stress placement in verbs and adjectives as follows:

$$Vw \rightarrow [\ 1\ stress\ ]\ /\ \left[\ \overline{\ +\ tense\ }\ \right] C_0\ ]_{VAdj}$$

This says to add primary stress on a vowel when it has the feature [ + tense ] and is followed by zero or more consonants and is at the end of a segment that is a verb or an adjective. For ultimate syllables containing lax vowels, we need the following rule:

$$\text{Vw} \rightarrow [\ 1\ \text{stress}\ ]\ /\ \underline{\qquad} C_0 \begin{bmatrix} + \text{voc} \\ - \text{cons} \\ - \text{tense} \end{bmatrix} C_0\ ]_{\text{VAdj}}$$

We will later need to add to these rules, but you should study how they operate now. The underline indicates the position in which the vowel with primary stress is found.

Before going further, apply these rules to the words listed below and check the results with your knowledge of English pronunciation:

| | | | |
|---|---|---|---|
| maroon | handsome | valid | corrode |
| compute | supreme | prohibit | imagine |

Now look at some more verbs and adjectives:

| | |
|---|---|
| defénd | compléx |
| remárk | rotúnd |
| resólve | abrúpt |
| regárd | corréct |
| subtráct | robúst |

According to our rules, all of these words should be stressed on the penultimate syllable, since they all have lax vowels in the ultimate syllables. If you look carefully at these words, however, you will notice that all end in two consonants. The adjective **complex**, which ends in /ks/, has primary stress on the penultimate syllable for some speakers; for others it is regular. None of the words we listed earlier ended in more than one consonant. We need to revise our rule:

1. $\text{Vw} \rightarrow [\ 1\ \text{stress}\ ]\ /\ \underline{\qquad} C_0\ [\ - \text{tense}\ ]\ C_0^1\ ]_{\text{VAdj}}$

2. $\text{Vw} \rightarrow [\ 1\ \text{stress}\ ]\ /\ \begin{bmatrix} \overline{\quad\quad} \\ + \text{tense} \end{bmatrix} C_0\ ]_{\text{VAdj}}$

3. $\text{Vw} \rightarrow [\ 1\ \text{stress}\ ]\ /\ \underline{\qquad} C_2\ ]_{\text{VAdj}}$

If the conditions of rule 1 are present, stress goes on the penultimate syllable; in all other cases it goes on the ultimate syllable.

In our syntactic rules we were often able to condense information. For example, we used braces to indicate a choice; if one element within the braces was chosen, the others were automatically excluded. In phonological rules we set an order on elements within braces. For

$$\begin{Bmatrix} a \\ b \\ c \end{Bmatrix}$$

we select $a$ if it meets our requirements and pass over $b$ and $c$. If $a$ does not meet our requirements, we select $b$ and omit $a$ and $c$. If neither $a$ nor $b$ fits, we select $c$. Our convention says that we must proceed from the top downward until we find a situation that applies; we then disregard other parts of the rule *even though other parts lower down may also apply*. With this convention, we can compress our three rules listed above into two: (a) rule 1 and (b) all other cases:

$$\text{Vw} \rightarrow [\ 1\ \text{stress}\ ]\ /\ \underline{\quad} \begin{Bmatrix} C_0 \begin{bmatrix} +\ \text{voc} \\ -\ \text{cons} \\ -\ \text{tense} \end{bmatrix} C_0^1 \\ C_0 \end{Bmatrix} ]_{\text{V Adj}}$$

Study the notation carefully. If a verb or an adjective ending in not more than one consonant has a lax vowel in the final syllable, primary stress is placed on the penultimate syllable. If this condition is met, we are not allowed to apply the second part of the rule. But if it is *not* met, primary stress is placed on the final syllable. Notice that verbs and adjectives of one syllable (**run, eat, blue, sad,** etc.) will never meet the conditions of the first rule, since they do not have penultimate syllables. The second rule will apply, then, assigning primary stress to their only syllables: rún, éat, blúe, sád.

We have used no words with derivational suffixes, such as **management** or **realize**; they will be treated later. Since most adverbs are formed by derivation, we will not discuss them here. Now let us look at some nouns:

| *1* | *2* | *3* |
|---|---|---|
| sýllable | amóeba | surrénder |
| élephant | móment | compléxion |
| metrópolis | halitósis | lántern |

If we omit the final syllable, these words follow the same pattern as do verbs and adjectives. In column 1, if we drop the final syllable of **metropolis,** we have **metropol-** with a lax vowel in the last syllable. Rule 1, therefore, assigns stress to the preceding syllable: metrópol-. Similarly, after dropping the last syllable in the words of column 2, we have a tense vowel in the new ultimate syllable: halitós-; in column 3 there will be two consonants ending the new final syllable: surrénd-.

We can augment our rule to allow for stress placement in nouns that have lax vowels in their final syllables:

$$
\text{M1: } Vw \rightarrow [\ 1 \text{ stress }] \ / \ \underline{\quad} \left\{ \begin{array}{l} C_0 \begin{bmatrix} + \text{ voc} \\ - \text{ cons} \\ - \text{ tense} \end{bmatrix} C_0^1 \\ C_0 \end{array} \right\} \quad \begin{array}{l} i \\ \\ ii \end{array}
$$

$$
/ \ \underline{\quad} \left\{ \begin{array}{l} \begin{bmatrix} + \text{ voc} \\ - \text{ cons} \\ - \text{ tense} \end{bmatrix} C_0 \ ]_N \\ ] \end{array} \right\} \quad \begin{array}{l} a \\ \\ b \end{array}
$$

This revision gives four possible patterns:

*a i* If the final syllable of a noun contains a lax vowel, this syllable is not used in determining stress placement. If the remainder of the word meets condition *i*, primary stress is placed on the penultimate syllable of the remainder (the antepenultimate syllable of the entire word): metrópol(is).

*a ii* If the final syllable of a noun contains a lax vowel, this syllable is not used in determining stress placement. If the remainder of the word ends in a syllable with a tense vowel or two or more consonants at the end, then stress is placed on the ultimate syllable of this remainder (the penultimate syllable of the entire word): amóe(ba).

*b i* If the word is not a noun ending in a syllable with a lax vowel, the final syllable must be considered. If the final syllable contains a lax vowel and ends in no more than one consonant, stress is placed on the penultimate syllable: explícit.

*b ii* If none of the above conditions is met, stress is placed on the final syllable: defénd, sublíme.

These rules apply in order; we must use the first one that is applicable and are not allowed to use any other.

Notice that a noun ending in a tense vowel does not meet condition *a i* or *a ii*; condition *b ii* is met for these words: ballóon, maríne, brocáde, etc.

Words of three or more syllables are often subject to another rule that adds a new stress. Anecdote receives primary stress on the last syllable since it contains a tense vowel: anecdóte (*b ii*). A new rule adds primary stress back two syllables: ánecdóte. By a special convention of phonology, any time we add a primary stress, all previously existing stresses are reduced by one. By this rule the last syllable of anecdote will reduce to secondary stress: ánecdôte. Here is the rule:

$$M2: \text{Vw} \rightarrow [\ 1\ \text{stress}\ ] \ / \ \underline{\hspace{1cm}}\ C_0 \begin{bmatrix} + \text{voc} \\ - \text{cons} \end{bmatrix} C_0 \begin{bmatrix} + \text{voc} \\ - \text{cons} \\ 1\ \text{stress} \end{bmatrix} C_0 \ ]_{\text{NVAdj}}$$

Let us follow this rule through with meditate. By M1, primary stress is placed on the final tense syllable: meditáte (b ii). By M2, primary stress is added two syllables back, and the already existing stress is reduced by one: méditâte. Notice how these rules apply to the following words:

|            |            |             |
|------------|------------|-------------|
| Farenheit  | isosceles  | pontificate |
| formaldehyde | escalate | corrugate   |
| satellite  | chloroform | pedigree    |

So far we have seen only how stress is added within words; let us now see what happens when words are combined into larger structures. The transformational rules can leave us with a surface structure like the following:

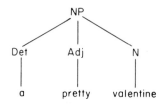

The words of this NP should be expressed in generalized phonological representations, but such abstract representations would be only confusing now. You can apply the stress placement rules with your knowledge of how the sounds in these words are pronounced in their final forms.

We can express the structural information given in the above tree in another form that is more convenient for placing stress:

$$[_{\text{NP}}\ a\ [_{\text{Adj}}\ \text{pretty}\ ]_{\text{Adj}}\ [_{\text{N}}\ \text{valentine}\ ]_{\text{N}}\ ]_{\text{NP}}$$

This labeled bracketing, like the tree, says that pretty is an adjective, valentine is a noun, and a pretty valentine is a noun phrase. We will establish a convention that determiners, auxiliaries, and prepositions are left unbracketed, since they are not stressed except for emphasis.

In its underlying form, the final vowel of **pretty** is lax. Rules M1 and M2 apply as follows:

M1 $[_{NP}$ a $[_{Adj}$ prétty $]_{Adj}$ $[_N$ valentíne $]_N$ $]_{NP}$

M2 $[_{NP}$ a $[_{Adj}$ prétty $]_{Adj}$ $[_N$ válentîne $]_N$ $]_{NP}$

After we have applied all the rules in the cycle, we erase innermost brackets and start over:

$[_{NP}$ a prétty válentîne $]_{NP}$

Since this is a structure larger than a word, M1 and M2 do not apply.

We are now ready for a new rule:

$$M3: Vw \rightarrow [\ 1\ stress\ ] / [\ X \left[ \overline{\underset{1\ stress}{\phantom{xxx}}} \right] Y\ ]$$

Condition 1: $Y$ contains no occurrences of [ 1 stress ].

Condition 2: The bracketed group is a phrase larger than a lexical category (N, V, Adj, etc.).

This rule tells us that within a bracketed phrase to add primary stress to the last vowel that already has primary stress; this rule has no noticeable effect on the vowel with primary stress, but it reduces all other stresses by one. By M3, **a prétty válentîne** will become **a prêtty válentìne**. Unstressed vowels are not marked. We now have three degrees of stress, listed in decreasing order of strength:

1. primary: ´
2. secondary: ˆ
3. tertiary: ˋ

You probably do not hear the difference between secondary and tertiary stress in **a pretty valentine**, although you should have no difficulty in recognizing primary and weak (i.e., unstressed). Eventually, with enough practice, you will hear all of these differences. Until then you can rely on the rules for marking stress.

Notice that rule M3 applies to any bracketed group, not just the noun phrase. It does not apply to lexical categories, such as N, V, etc. The VP **bought a pencil** will receive stress as follows:

M1 $[_{VP}$ past $[_{MV}$ $[_V$ búy $]_V$ $[_{NP}$ a $[_N$ péncil $]_N$ $]_{NP}$ $]_{MV}$ $]_{VP}$

Rule M2 does not apply since its conditions are not met, and M3 applies only to structures larger than the word. We now erase the innermost brackets and start the cycle of rules over again:

$$[_{VP} \text{ past } [_{MV} [_V \text{ búy } ]_V [_{NP} \text{ a péncil } ]_{NP} ]_{MV} ]_{VP}$$

Notice that we are following a process similar to that which we used with transformations in embedded structures. Elements within innermost brackets are parallel to the most deeply embedded S. We now go through our cycle of transformations again. Again M1 applies, but it does not alter the stress pattern, since there is only one stressed vowel in each bracketed structure. Since M2 and M3 do not apply, we again erase brackets and start over on our cycle:

$$[_{VP} \text{ past } [_{MV} \text{ búy a péncil } ]_{MV} ]_{VP}$$

M1 and M2 are inapplicable now, but M3 assigns primary stress to the first syllable of **pencil** and reduces all other stresses by one:

$$\text{M3 } [_{VP} \text{ past } [_{MV} \text{ bùy a péncil } ]_{MV} ]_{VP}$$

Since tense is not subject to stress, we erase the MV brackets and do not apply the cycle further:

$$[_{VP} \text{ past bùy a péncil } ]_{VP}$$

If we have an entire sentence, such as **Janice bought a pencil**, we would follow the same steps as we did for **bought a pencil**:

$$[_S [_{NP} \text{ Jánice } ]_{NP} [_{VP} \text{ past bùy a péncil } ]_{VP} ]_S$$

Removing innermost brackets, we have

$$[_S \text{ Jánice past bùy a péncil } ]_S$$
$$\text{M3 } [_S \text{ Jânice past bùy a péncil } ]_S$$

After converting *past + buy* to **bought** and erasing the final brackets, we have **Jânice bòught a péncil**. Notice that rule M3 applies to any bracketed group larger than a lexical category: AP, VP, NP, S, etc.

If a word is pronounced in isolation, it functions as a sentence:

$$[_S [_{NP} \text{ cavalcade } ]_{NP} ]_S$$
$$\text{M1 } [_S [_{NP} \text{ cavalcáde } ]_{NP} ]_S$$
$$\text{M2 } [_S [_{NP} \text{ cávalcâde } ]_{NP} ]_S$$
$$\text{M3 } [_S \text{ cávalcàde } ]_S$$

Hence, no word pronounced in isolation will ever have secondary stress.

For any new sentence that we create, we are automatically able to assign the correct stress pattern; stress placement in the individual's internalized grammar is, therefore, determined by rules. For new words we normally have the same proficiency. Rules M1, M2, and M3 are an elementary attempt at accounting for this ability.

## exercises

A.  Use rules M1 and M2 to determine the stress placement for the following words:

| | | | |
|---|---|---|---|
| 1. adapt | 7. synopsis | 13. achieve | 19. hypotenuse |
| 2. sturdy | 8. antelope | 14. arsenal | 20. devote |
| 3. analysis | 9. arena | 15. matador | 21. neophyte |
| 4. anecdote | 10. complete | 16. appendix | 22. determine |
| 5. remote | 11. baritone | 17. certain | 23. horizon |
| 6. elect | 12. cancel | 18. robust | 24. mediate |

B.  Apply the cycle of transformations M1, M2, and M3 as many times as needed to give the stress placement on the following sentences:

1. Terry stayed sound asleep.
2. The cook baked a cake.
3. Gwendolyn has frightened Frankenstein.
4. An ugly woman drank the lethal gasoline.
5. Elizabeth spoke in a monotone.

# chapter seventeen
# STRESS AND PITCH

In the last chapter we avoided stress placement in words like **writer**, **lovely**, **familiarize**, and **management**. Each of these is derived from another word: **write**, **love**, **familiar**, **manage**. We speak of a suffix (**-er**, **-ly**, **-ize**, **-ment**) that is used to derive one word from another as a **derivational suffix**. In most cases the derived word belongs to a different part of speech from the original (**write** is a verb, **writer** a noun), but not always (both **host** and **hostess** are nouns).

Most dictionaries list derived words as separate entries from the words they are based on. For the kind of lexicon proposed by transformationalists, this procedure is uneconomical and ignores significant generalizations about English. For example, the agentive suffix **-er** (also spelled **-or**) means one who performs an act, regardless of which verb it is attached to. Column 1 below gives the kind of listing normally found in dictionaries; column 2 shows the kind we are suggesting. Imagine each word with a full lexical entry: definition, phonological form, and idiosyncratic features.

|  *1*  |  *2*  |
|-------|-------|
| act | act |
| actor | -er |
| govern | govern |
| governor | play |
| play | write |
| player | |
| write | |
| writer | |

This limited listing should be enough to suggest the tremendous saving that will be achieved by not listing derived forms that are predictable by rule, especially when we consider the thousands of verbs in the language to which this suffix may be added. More important than the saving of space are the generalizations that rules such as one for adding agentive suffixes will provide. A native speaker of English who learns a new verb, such as the possible **flate**, will understand the noun **flator** the first time he encounters it, or he might introduce it himself without realizing that he is creating anything new. The procedure of listing derivatives as separate entries does not show how this process is possible; the rule we are suggesting does. Since an adequate grammar should approach as closely as possible the native speaker's knowledge of his language, this is an important generalization. Our process shows the relationship between **actor** and other words with agentive suffixes; these relationships are unquestionably accounted for by the individual's internalized grammar.

The procedure we are suggesting will be used with all derivational suffixes, as well as with derivational prefixes (**enjoy**, **devalue**, **unreasonable**, etc.). Prefixes and suffixes together are known as *affixes*. The lexical entry for each affix will include full information on which words it may be added to. This information whenever possible will be given in terms of features.

Because languages are systematic, we frequently see repetition of patterns, such as the WH rule for questions, relative clauses, and noun clauses. Whenever a generalization in one part of the grammar leads to simplifications of other parts, we know that we have formulated a significant generalization. In the last chapter we saw that our treatment of syntax enables us to give a correct placement of stress patterns on words and sentences. Such classifications as N, V, Adj, NP, VP, etc., enable us to give stress placement by rule rather than by individual markings on each word in the lexicon. This process is parallel to the individual's knowledge of how to place stresses on a sentence he is creating for the first time and his knowledge of how most new words he reads should be pronounced. The concept of ordered transformational rules that operate in a cycle from the most deeply embedded element upward is found again in the rules for stress.

This cyclic principle applies to derived words as well as to noun phrases and sentences. **Personal** will be given on a tree diagram as

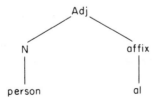

or with a labeled bracketing as

$$[_{Adj} \ [_N \ \text{person} \ ]_N \ \text{al} \ ]_{Adj}$$

We begin with the word within the innermost brackets, the noun **person**, and use all applicable rules:

M1 [$_N$ pérson ]$_N$

Since this is a noun, the final syllable with a lax vowel is passed over for stress placement purposes; since there is only one other syllable, the stress must fall on it. This word is too short for M2 to apply, so we erase the innermost brackets and begin the cycle again for the adjective **personal**. An addition to rule M1 would direct us to treat derivational adjectival affixes with lax vowels the same as we do final syllables in nouns: disregard them for stress purposes.

M1 [$_{Adj}$ pérsonal ]$_{Adj}$

After marking off the derivational affix, we have a lax vowel followed by only one consonant in the last syllable of the remainder of the word: **person(al)**; hence, stress goes on the first syllable.

Look now at **personality**:

[$_N$ [$_{Adj}$ [$_N$ person ]$_N$ al ]$_{Adj}$ ity ]$_N$

The first two cycles will apply as we have already stated:

M1 pérson (noun)

M1 pérsonal (adjective)

Now we erase the next set of brackets and have the noun **personality**. The last syllable is dropped from consideration; the penultimate contains a lax vowel followed by a single consonant. The stress falls, then, on the antepenultimate syllable, and the previously existing stress is weakened by one:

M1 pêrsonálity

In a sentence further application of the rules will, of course, reduce the secondary stress, as in **Her personality is pleasing**:

[$_S$ [$_{NP}$ her pêrsonálity ]$_{NP}$ [$_{VP}$ is pléasing ]$_{VP}$ ]$_S$

Erasing innermost brackets and applying rule M3, we get

[$_S$ her pèrsonâlity is pléasing ]$_S$

You will notice that most determiners, auxiliaries, prepositions, and pronouns are not stressed.

For most words such as **telegraph** and **telescope**, if we remove the prefix, we are left with an element that does not fit easily into any of our lexical categories (N, V, Adj). Although we do have the words **graph** and **scope** as nouns in English, these do not seem to be the stem to which **tele-** has been added, although they are etymologically related. We will refer to **graph** and **scope** in **telegraph** and **telescope** as **stems**. Stress is placed on **telescope** as follows:

$$[_N \text{ tele } [_{stem} \text{ scope }]_{stem}]_N$$
$$\text{M1 } [_N \text{ tele } [_{stem} \text{ scópe }]_{stem}]_N$$
$$\text{M1 } [_N \text{ telescópe }]_N$$
$$\text{M2 } [_N \text{ télescôpe }]_N$$

Words such as **telegraph** and **telescope** receive stress placement by the same cyclic principles as other words with prefixes or suffixes.

Our treatment of stress placement has been illustrative and far from exhaustive. A complete discussion of stress in English would require a book at least the length of this one, and there are still many unanswered questions. Our purpose has been to show you how stress rules operate and to relate them to the rest of the grammar.

Interacting with stress is pitch, the relative highness or lowness of a sound. Each person has a normal pitch level from which he varies upward or downward to provide variation. If he speaks in falsetto or some other manner not usual for him, he sets up a new "normal" pitch level. In speaking of pitch in language, we are talking about *relative* pitch—the variation from the norm—not *absolute* pitch as in music. A person's normal level is given the number 2; variation below that level is given the number 1, and anything above it the number 3. Most phonologists give a fourth level for extra high pitch; this level is found only in rare cases, such as excitement, and will not be included in the discussion that follows.

The rules for stress placement will assign the following patterns:

1. Bîll wènt físhing.
2. Frân ròde to tówn.
3. Rây sàw Fréddy.
4. Rây sáw him.

For normal speech that does not give special emphasis to any word or show contrast, you begin each of these sentences at the level that is normal for you. You continue with this pitch level until you reach the word with primary stress; then you rise to the third level and immediately afterward drop below your normal level to level 1 and fade out. Pitch numbers are placed before the syllables to which they apply:

1. $^2$Bîll wènt $^3$físh$^1$ing

2. $^2$Frân ròde to $^3$tówn$^1$

3. $^2$Rây sàw $^3$Fréd$^1$dy

4. $^2$Rây sàw Frèddy $^3$Ád$^1$ams

5. $^2$Rây $^3$sáw $^1$him

In sentence 1 since **fishing** contains two syllables and is stressed on the first, the change from the third to the first pitch level occurs between syllables and causes no distortion of the word. In sentence 2, however, this change occurs on the monosyllabic word **town**, producing a "drawling" effect. Contrast this pronunciation of **town** with that in **Fran rode to town yésterday**. Sentences 3 and 4 illustrate the combination of primary stress and third level pitch on the last syllable of the sentence.

The yes/no question has a different pitch pattern from the affirmative sentence:

1. $^2$Did she $^3$án$^3$swer

2. $^2$Are you $^3$gó$^3$ing

3. $^2$Was she $^3$súre$^3$

As with the affirmative sentence, you start off on the normal second pitch level and rise to level 3 on the syllable with primary stress. Instead of falling to level 1 and fading off, you fade off from level 3.

Notice that WH questions do not have the same pitch pattern as yes/no questions:

1. $^2$Where are you $^3$gó$^1$ing

2. $^2$What did you $^3$sée$^1$

3. $^2$When'll you be $^3$réa$^1$dy

WH questions follow the /2 3 1/ pattern of the affirmative sentence. This difference in pitch pattern gives us further support for distinguishing yes/no and WH questions in addition to their differences in structure.

Deviations from the normal stress or pitch pattern cau e a change in the meaning of the sentence:

1. Jóhn said not to go
2. John sáid not to go
3. John said nót to go
4. ²John said not to ³go³
5. ²Where am I ³go³ing
6. ²This cake is ³good³

The first three sentences have primary stress on words that would normally not receive it, thereby giving special emphasis to certain words and additional implied meaning. Sentences 4 and 5 are paraphrases of **Did John say not to go?** and **Did you ask where I am going?** Sentence 6 is a typical kind of sarcastic question. Since these deviations from normal stress and pitch patterns cause changes in meaning, they must be indicated in the deep structure with morphemes similar to Q so that the semantic component can give the sentences their correct meaning.

The sentences we have illustrated so far have been short ones that are normally uttered fairly rapidly with no pauses for breath. Examine a longer sentence:

²Those old trunks in the ³át²tic ²contain many sur³prís¹es

Notice that there is a primary stress on **attic** with a corresponding rise in pitch; the pitch level does not fall to 1, but returns to 2 and remains until **surprises**, where it again rises with the primary stress and falls to level 1. The pattern /2 3 2/ in **those old trunks in the attic** shows that the structure is not complete; the /2 3 1/ pattern of **contain many surprises** does indicate completion. We call a structure containing one primary stress accompanied by a rise in pitch a **phonological phrase**. The sentence we illustrated contains two phonological phrases; for short sentences, the entire sentence is one phonological phrase. Phonological phrases are partially determined by breathing habits, partially by syntactic patterns. In the sentence above, the break between the two phrases comes between the NP and the VP, a normal breaking point when the NP is long. Nonrestrictive modifiers occur as phonological phrases separate from the rest of the sentence. Any long sentence contains several phonological phrases.

There is probably some well-defined relationship between phonological phrases and syntactic patterns. This is an area of phonology that has hardly been examined in the past. Rules for phonological phrases and pitch patterns will probably be placed in the phonological component of future grammars, near rules for stress. All of the transformational rules must have been applied and the pattern of the surface structure been defined before any of the phonological rules can operate. Future research will probably tell us something about junctures, or pauses. Current beliefs about junctures have been severely challenged, but there has been nothing yet to replace them.

## exercises

A. Use rules M1 and M2 to mark the stress patterns in the following words:

| | | | |
|---|---|---|---|
| 1. inert | 7. beautiful | 13. universal | 19. telephone |
| 2. lurid | 8. morose | 14. incidental | 20. telegraphic |
| 3. habit | 9. escape | 15. designate | 21. pomposity |
| 4. habitual | 10. pompadour | 16. circumstance | 22. traumatic |
| 5. public | 11. blanket | 17. character | 23. Palestine |
| 6. serene | 12. adjectival | 18. momentous | 24. equatorial |

B. Use rules M1, M2, and M3 to place stress on the following phrases and sentences:
1. an insipid circumstance
2. an academic teacher
3. a superb holiday
4. The chicken crossed the road.
5. The operator separated the customers.

C. Mark primary stress and pitch levels:
1. The hunters shot a rhinoceros.
2. Where did you see it?
3. Weren't you frightened?
4. Those deplorable performances caused the theater to be closed.
5. Frank Ibsen, who won first prize last year, isn't entering the contest.
6. My idea is agreeable?
7. Because we couldn't see for the heavy fog, we stopped driving.
8. When did you get married?
9. Wasn't the old woman on the back row about to fall asleep?
10. The troops seemed restless.

D. It would be possible to define a sentence as an utterance with one pitch pattern that is /2 3 1/ or /2 3 3/. Discuss the effectiveness of this definition.

E. Give several reasons for making the division indicated by 1 rather than 2:
1. All the people in the audience / heard what he said.
2. All the people in the audience heard / what he said.

# chapter eighteen
## *PHONOLOGICAL RULES*

In the last chapter we saw that for most words in English, stress is predictable by rules. Since the lexicon lists only idiosyncratic features, stress will be given only for those lexical entries that are exceptions. The stress-placement rules permit us to see a system in our language that would be totally obscured if we merely specified the stress for each word in the lexicon.

Another regular phonological process is the formation of plurals for most English nouns. Since the same rules apply for both noun plurals and for third-person singular present-tense verbs, we group the rules together:

$$\text{M4: present} + V \rightarrow V + \begin{bmatrix} + \text{anterior} \\ + \text{coronal} \\ + \text{strident} \end{bmatrix}$$

Rule M4 rewrites present plus a verb as that verb plus a segment that is [ + anterior, + coronal, + strident ]. You will notice that this describes the natural class which includes /s/ and /z/. Another name for a class such as this is **archisegment**. The lexical entries for have, be, do, and say, as well as those for the modals, will block the application of this rule for them.

We next consider the morpheme we have indicated merely as Pl:

$$\text{M5: Pl} \rightarrow \begin{bmatrix} + \text{anterior} \\ + \text{coronal} \\ + \text{strident} \end{bmatrix}$$

Up to this point the grammar has kept the verb singular ending s (eats, sits, etc.) separate from the plural ending because they are different morphemes with different meanings. Now they can both be stated as the same archisegment.

$$\text{M6: } \varnothing \rightarrow \begin{bmatrix} + \text{voc} \\ + \text{high} \\ - \text{back} \\ - \text{tense} \end{bmatrix} \Big/ \begin{bmatrix} + \text{strident} \\ + \text{coronal} \end{bmatrix} \underline{\hspace{1cm}} \begin{bmatrix} + \text{anterior} \\ + \text{coronal} \\ + \text{strident} \end{bmatrix}$$

Rule M6 adds /ɪ/ if the archisegment follows a segment that is [ + strident ] and [ + coronal ].

We now need a rule that will convert the archisegment specifically into /s/ or /z/:

$$\text{M7:} \quad \begin{bmatrix} + \text{anterior} \\ + \text{coronal} \\ + \text{strident} \end{bmatrix} \rightarrow [\; \alpha \text{ voice} \;] \; / \; [\; \alpha \text{ voice} \;] \; \underline{\quad\quad}$$

Since rules M4 through M7 are numbered, they apply in order. Rule M7 now makes the feature [ voice ] on the archisegment agree with this feature on the preceding segment. The symbol **alpha** means that the feature can be plus or minus, but that all alphas in one rule will be consistently the same. If the segment before the archisegment has the feature [ + voice ], then the archisegment becomes /z/; if the preceding segment has [ − voice ], then the archisegment becomes /s/.

With these rules, the following derivations are possible. We are using alphabetic abbreviations for all segments except those that are being added so that you can concentrate on the application of the rules more easily.

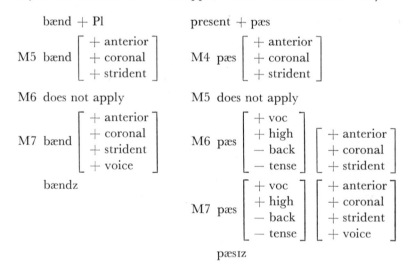

Another pair of regular formations are past tense and past participle in words such as **drop, dropped, dropped**. All other formations will be listed as exceptions in the lexicon and will block the application of the following rules:

$$\text{M8:} \quad \begin{Bmatrix} \text{past} \\ \text{en} \end{Bmatrix} + V \rightarrow V + \begin{bmatrix} - \text{continuant} \\ - \text{nasal} \\ + \text{anterior} \\ + \text{coronal} \end{bmatrix}$$

Rule M8 replaces **past** and **en** with an archisegment that includes /t/ and /d/ and moves it after the verb.

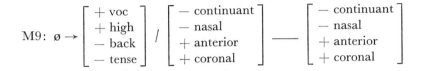

$$
\text{M9:} \quad \emptyset \rightarrow
\begin{bmatrix} + \text{voc} \\ + \text{high} \\ - \text{back} \\ - \text{tense} \end{bmatrix}
/
\begin{bmatrix} - \text{continuant} \\ - \text{nasal} \\ + \text{anterior} \\ + \text{coronal} \end{bmatrix}
\underline{\qquad}
\begin{bmatrix} - \text{continuant} \\ - \text{nasal} \\ + \text{anterior} \\ + \text{coronal} \end{bmatrix}
$$

Rule M9 adds /ɪ/ if the archisegment follows /t/ or /d/.

$$
\text{M10:} \quad
\begin{bmatrix} - \text{continuant} \\ - \text{nasal} \\ + \text{anterior} \\ + \text{coronal} \end{bmatrix}
\rightarrow [\ \alpha \text{ voice}\ ] \ / \ [\ \alpha \text{ voice}\ ] \ \underline{\qquad}
$$

Rule M10 makes the archisegment agree in voice with the segment that precedes it.

The next rule can be simplified by the use of alphabetic abbreviations for the complexes of features:

$$
\text{M11:} \quad \text{ing} + V \rightarrow V + \text{ɪŋ}
$$

This, of course, is the rule that gives the present participial symbol **ing** a phonological form and attaches it after the verb. This rule is very simple since there is no variation in its application.

We need a rule for vowels that have not received stress by the stress rules M1 through M3:

$$
\text{M12:} \quad
\begin{bmatrix} + \text{voc} \\ - \text{cons} \\ - \text{stress} \\ - \text{tense} \end{bmatrix}
\rightarrow \text{ə}
$$

Any vowel that has not received stress by our rules has the feature [ − stress ]. All unstressed lax vowels reduce to /ə/, the sound of the vowel in the last syllable of **batter, Cuba, pleasure,** etc. This is a generalized form of all vowels that are lax and unstressed and was, therefore, not listed in our inventory of vowels in earlier chapters. There is much dialectal variation in the actual performance of this vowel, since it also may occur as a higher vowel similar to /ɪ/. More sophisticated rules would, of course, take care of these variations.

So far we have said little about the way morphemes will be entered in the lexicon except that they will be stated in features with all redundancies omitted. We also said that derived forms such as **actor** and **personality** will not be included, since they can be predicted by rules and the entries for derivational affixes. We run into a problem on citation forms, since many words vary in pronunciation according to the environment. For example, we could enter **photograph** as /fotəgræf/ and encounter no difficulties with the word in such combinations as **photograph equipment** or in the derivative **photographic**. When we try to derive **photographer**, however, we have a problem:

> citation form: fotəgræf
>
> derivation:     fətagrəfər

We can easily arrive at /ə/ in the unstressed vowels of the derivation by rule M12, but there is no way we can predict /a/ if we have /ə/ in the citation form, since /ə/ is the reduced form for all vowels. We will say that /ə/ cannot appear in any citation forms and that its only source is rule M12. Instead of /fotəgræf/ as the citation form, we will use /fotagræf/ and call it a **deep phonological form**. Since deep syntactic structures are often radically different from surface structures, it should not be surprising that deep phonological forms are different from those on the surface.

The study of deep phonology has barely begun. Some linguists are advancing convincing reasons for using deep forms that are very similar to regular English spelling. These forms will be the same for all dialects of English, all differences being accounted for by phonological rules. The phonological rules, in turn, can be applied only after the structure of the sentence, its basic syntax, has been established. Because so little is known about deep phonology, we have limited our goal in this last chapter to giving you some understanding of the role that rules play in transforming deep phonological forms into surface forms.

We have studied the interrelatedness of syntax, semantics, and phonology. It is the syntactic component that is central to transformational grammar, since the other two are dependent on it. Only the syntactic component can create new structures without limit. Semantics and phonology merely assign meaning and form to an abstract structure. The general principles we apply in transforming deep syntactic structures into surface structures hold true in the phonological component as well, and we suspect that they will also prove applicable to the semantic component when research in that field is more advanced.

## exercises

A. Apply rules M4–M7 to the following:

    1. joke + Pl    4. pig + Pl    7. present + pitch    10. present + grab
    2. judge + Pl    5. wish + Pl    8. present + laugh
    3. bat + Pl    6. present + rip    9. present + please

B. Apply rules M8–M11 to the following:

    1. past + stop    5. past + close    9. ing + eat
    2. en + stab    6. en + seed    10. past + open
    3. en + test    7. past + marry
    4. ing + go    8. past + wait

C. Why are the and a normally pronounced /ðə/ and /ə/ instead of /ði/ and /e/? What pronunciation do you give was in He was going?

D. Prepare rules to account for the phonological changes found in the following words:

    1. advocate, advocacy; pirate, piracy; complacent, complacency (/t/ and /s/)
    2. soft, soften; haste, hasten; moist, moisten (/t/)

E. Show how a transformational grammar produces the sentence The little girls cried. Apply all relevant rules in each of the components of the grammar.

# BIBLIOGRAPHY

This bibliography is restricted to those works which will be of greatest interest to the reader of this book in giving fuller accounts of the grammar and in presenting viewpoints different from those found in this book. Most of the full-length works contain more detailed bibliographies.

Bach, Emmon, *An Introduction to Transformational Grammars*. New York: Holt, Rinehart and Winston, 1964.

Bach, Emmon, and Robert T. Harms, eds., *Universals in Linguistic Theory*. New York: Holt, Rinehart and Winston, 1968.

Bolinger, Dwight, "The Atomization of Meaning," *Language*, XLI (1965), 555–73.

Chomsky, Noam, *Aspects of the Theory of Syntax*. Cambridge, Mass.: MIT Press, 1965.

———, "Current Issues in Linguistic Theory," in *The Structure of Language*, ed. Jerry A. Fodor and Jerrold J. Katz. Englewood Cliffs, N.J.: Prentice-Hall, Inc., 1964.

———, "Some General Properties of Phonological Rules," *Language*, XLIII (1967), 102–28.

———, "Some Methodological Remarks on Generative Grammar," *Word*, XVII (1961), 219–39.

———, *Syntactic Structures*. 's-Gravenhage: Mouton and Co., 1957.

———, "A Transformational Approach to Syntax," in *Third Texas Conference on Problems of Linguistic Analysis in English, 1958*, ed. Archibald A. Hill. Austin: University of Texas Press, 1962.

Chomsky, Noam, and Morris Halle, *The Sound Pattern of English*. New York: Harper and Row, 1968.

Fillmore, Charles J., "The Position of Embedding Transformations in a Grammar," *Word*, XIX (1963), 208–31.

Gleason, H. A., Jr., *Linguistics and English Grammar*. New York: Holt, Rinehart and Winston, 1965.

Halle, Morris, "On the Bases of Phonology," *Il Nuovo Cimento*, XIII, Series X (supplement) (1958), 494–517. Repr. in *The Structure of Language*, ed. Jerry A. Fodor and Jerrold J. Katz. Englewood Cliffs, N.J.: Prentice-Hall, Inc., 1964.

Halle, Morris, "Phonology in Generative Grammar," *Word*, XVIII (1962), 54–72. Repr. in *The Structure of Language*, ed. Jerry A. Fodor and Jerrold J. Katz. Englewood Cliffs, N.J.: Prentice-Hall, Inc., 1964.

Harms, Robert T., *Introduction to Phonological Theory*. Englewood Cliffs, N.J.: Prentice-Hall, Inc., 1968.

Jacobs, Roderick A., and Peter S. Rosenbaum, *English Transformational Grammar*. Waltham, Mass.: Blaisdell Publishing Company, 1968.

Katz, Jerrold J., and Jerry A. Fodor, "The Structure of a Semantic Theory," *Language* XXXIX (1963), 170–210. Repr. in *The Structure of Language*, ed. Jerry A. Fodor and Jerrold J. Katz. Englewood Cliffs, N.J.: Prentice-Hall, Inc., 1964.

Katz, Jerrold J., and Paul M. Postal, *An Integrated Theory of Linguistic Descriptions*. Cambridge, Mass.: MIT Press, 1964.

Klima, Edward S., "Negation in English," in *The Structure of Language*, ed. Jerry A. Fodor and Jerrold J. Katz. Englewood Cliffs, N.J.: Prentice-Hall, Inc., 1964.

Langacker, Ronald W., *Language and Its Structure*. New York: Harcourt, Brace, and World, Inc., 1968.

Langendoen, D. Terence, *The Study of Syntax*. New York: Holt, Rinehart and Winston, Inc., 1969.

Lees, Robert B., *The Grammar of English Nominalizations*. Research Center in Anthropology, Folklore, and Linguistics, Publication No. 12. Bloomington, Indiana: Indiana University Press, 1960.

———, "Grammatical Analysis of the English Comparative Construction," *Word*, XVII (1961), 171–85.

Lees, Robert B., and Edward S. Klima, "Rules for English Pronominalization," *Language*, XXXIX (1963), 17–28.

Postal, Paul M., *Aspects of Phonological Theory*. New York: Harper and Row, 1968.

Reibel, David A., and Sanford A. Schane, *Modern Studies in English*. Englewood Cliffs, N.J.: Prentice-Hall, Inc., 1969.

Smith, Carlota S., "A Class of Complex Modifiers in English," *Language*, XXXVII (1961), 342–365.

———, "Determiners and Relative Clauses in a Generative Grammar of English," *Language*, XL (1964), 37–52.

Stanley, Richard, "Redundancy Rules in Phonology," *Language*, XLIII (1967), 393–436.

Stockwell, Robert P., "The Place of Intonation in a Generative Grammar of English," *Language*, XXXVI (1960), 360–67.

Thomas, Owen, *Transformational Grammar and the Teacher of English*. New York: Holt, Rinehart and Winston, Inc., 1965.

# INDEX

TEXAS WOMANS UNIVERSITY
LIBRARY